this & that

10 knits to keep you warm and cozy

quince&co.

Quince & Co
quinceandco.com

First edition

ISBN 978-0-9979187-5-5

Printed in the United States.

contents

introduction

Cables, colorwork, textures in harmony—this is the staff of knitting life. The ten pieces in this book incorporate these classic techniques in otherwise easy, unfussy pieces. They are the follow up to the simple stitch work and stripped-down basic sweaters featured in *Plain & Simple*, the prequel to this book.

Like the projects in the first book, the ones here are meant to be inviting both in the making and in the wearing—comfort knitting for experienced knitters, confidence building for new ones. These are sweaters to put on first thing in the morning and to take off last thing at night. Although they feature more advanced knitting moves—working two colors in a row, crossing stitches for cables, mixing knits, purls and sometimes yarnovers—by and large, they don't require having to pay attention to too many things *at the same time* (that dreaded phrase in knitting patterns).

As before, many of the sweaters in *This & That* use one of my favorite sweater constructions, a modified dolman sleeve, more fitted and set higher under the arm than traditional dolmans. There are also traditional round-yoke pieces, oversize shapes and snug ones, full, floaty sleeves and skinny; twisted stitches, honeycomb, and slipped stitches, as well as textures and cables; and there are two chunky, Bohus-inspired colorwork yokes, a Norwegian-style knock off, and a dress (!).

I immensely enjoyed swatching stitch ideas for the sweaters in this book. It was a delight to page through my stitch dictionaries, sampling this pattern and that, imagining how one might build them into a knitted piece, and it was fun to futz around with different color combinations.

That said, after the swatching phase comes the work of applying sample to sweater. I wouldn't be exaggerating to say that most of the pieces in this book have been ripped out and reknitted at least once to get them right. Such is the price of working stitch by stitch. But such is the pleasure, too, in a craft that never ceases to invite renewal. I hope very much that one or more of these pieces invites you to cast on. And perhaps to do a little swatching and designing of your own.

Pam

a word about owl

The sweaters in this book were designed mostly in Owl, a yarn from Quince & Co. Not that these pieces can't be made in other yarns. They most certainly can. But design and yarn go hand and hand, and Owl's loft and gentle heathered hues contribute greatly to the look and feel of these sweaters. Not to mention that every time I put needles to this lovely blend of wool and alpaca, I'm reminded how much a good yarn contributes to the pleasures of knitting. In addition to its hand, I love Owl's color palette. It comes in several undyed shades, earthy colors right from the fleece that I never tire of. Overdyed, the yarn makes wonderful heathered colors, soft and subtle or deep, rich, jewel toned.

New to this book is Owlet, a single-ply alpaca/wool that opens into lovely bloom as you knit. I fell in love with its airy hand when I worked on *Sweetfern*, a dress, and *Honeysuckle*, a sweater with gathers (opposite). It's a fine yarn, yes, but due to its halo, it can be worked on a large needle (I used a size US 8), so the Owlet pieces move along more quickly than you'd expect.

A word on color variation in the yarns from batch to batch. Undyed alpaca fiber comes in 22 different shades, blue-black through brown-black, cool-to-warm browns, fawn, white, silver-grey, and rose-grey, all in various lights and darks—these are the colors right off the animal. Strict duplication from dyelot to dyelot is impossible. A bale of true black alpaca one year might be closer to a deep charcoal the next. Working with natural fibers means having to embrace change and variation. I'm learning to celebrate nature's lack of consistency.

Owl holds a special place in my heart for another reason. Anyone who's worked with alpaca knows just how lovely, warm, and soft it can be. But possibly, in your own experience with alpaca, you may also have experienced its propensity to hang—and hang and hang—stretching down in the direction of your shoes. This isn't a problem inherent in the fiber. It's a spinning outcome. Alpaca is a hollow fiber, which means that there's air in the core. How much air you squeeze out or encourage in makes all the difference in the final yarn. In worsted spinning the fibers are aligned parallel to each other and squeezed together; that's what makes worsted yarns so lovely and even. But, in the case of alpaca, you end up with a soft but lank and drapey yarn. However, if you spin alpaca on what's called a woolen system, one that throws the fibers together willy-nilly and leaves the air for cushion between them, then you have a soft yarn buoyant and light; add wool to the mix for elasticity and bounce, and you welcome Owl and little Owlet.

Six pullovers,

two cardigans,

one dress,

and a hat

sweetfern

yarn: owlet
color: elf

bayberry

yarn: owl
colors: elf
sokoke
taiga
lagoon
yucca
straits

elderberry

yarn: owl
color: albertine

honeysuckle

yarn: owlet
color: tawny

BREATHE

sumac

yarn: owl
color: abyssinian

hobblebush

yarn: owl
colors: bubo
snowy
barred
steppe
allagash

winterberry

yarn: owl
colors: barents sea
elf
steppe

witch hazel

yarn: owl
color: steppe

buttonbush

yarn: owl
color: allagash

snowberry

yarn: owl
colors: albertine
snowy
barred
steppe
allagash

patterns

sweetfern

I've been wanting to make a dress like this for a long time. A light-as-air dress, warm and cozy. I took the bodice motifs directly from Barbara Walker's *A Treasury of Knitting Patterns* (Schoolhouse Press, 1998). The center panel is called Palm-Tree Puff. The puffs are threaded together with a column of pronounced knit stitches. The leaves, outlined in part by yarnovers, are titled Quilted Leaf. The original instructions have you twist the stitches in the leaf, but I opted not to, preserving softness.

Finished measurements
33¼ (37½, 41¾, 46, 50, 54¼, 58½, 62¾, 67)" [84.5 (95.5, 106, 117, 127, 138, 148.5, 159.5, 170) cm] bust circumference; shown in size 37½" [95.5 cm] on a 31" [79 cm], 5'11" [180 cm] tall model (6½" [16.5 cm] positive ease)

Yarn
Owlet by Quince & Co
(50% American wool, 50% alpaca; 240yd [220m]/50g)

- 9 (10, 11, 12, 13, 15, 16, 17, 18) skeins Elf 303

Needles

- One 16" circular needle (circ) in size US 5 [3.75 mm]
- One 32" circ in size US 7 [4.5 mm]
- One spare circ in size US 7 [4.5 mm]
- One set double-pointed needles (dpns) in size US 5 [3.75 mm]
- One set dpns in size US 7 [4.5 mm]

Or size to obtain gauge

Notions

- Stitch markers
- Waste yarn
- Tapestry needle
- Locking stitch marker

Embarking on a knitted dress is a commitment. But the work is easily broken into chunks. Work a quilted leaf at each sitting and before you know it, you're at the shoulder. For the skirt, work a set number of rounds at each sitting (find a great series on Netflix or listen to a lengthy good book to keep you company). You WILL get to the end.

Gauge
19 sts and 30 rnds = 4" [10 cm] in stockinette stitch with larger needle, after light steam blocking.

Palm leaf panel A (begins and ends as 1 st)
See also chart, page 58.
Worked in the rnd
Rnd 1: K1.
Rnds 2-10: Rep Rnd 1.
Rnd 11: Yo, k1, yo—3 sts.
Rnd 12: Yo, k3, yo—5 sts.
Rnd 13: Yo, k5, yo—7 sts.
Rnd 14: Yo, k7, yo—9 sts.
Rnd 15: Yo, k9, yo—11 sts.
Rnd 16: Ssk, k7, k2tog—9 sts.
Rnd 17: Ssk, k5, k2tog—7 sts.
Rnd 18: Ssk, k3, k2tog—5 sts.
Rnd 19: Ssk, k1, k2tog—3 sts.
Rnd 20: Sk2p—1 st.
Repeat Rnds 1-20 for palm leaf panel A in the rnd.

Worked flat
Row 1: (RS) K1.
Row 2: P1.
Rows 3-10: Rep Rows 1 and 2 four times.
Row 11: (RS) Yo, k1, yo—3 sts.
Row 12: Yo, p3, yo—5 sts.
Row 13: Yo, k5, yo—7 sts.
Row 14: Yo, p7, yo—9 sts.
Row 15: Yo, k9, yo—11 sts.
Row 16: P2tog, p7, ssp—9 sts.
Row 17: Ssk, k5, k2tog—7 sts.
Row 18: P2tog, p3, ssp—5 sts.
Row 19: Ssk, k1, k2tog—3 sts.
Row 20: P3tog-tbl—1 sts.
Repeat Rows 1-20 for palm leaf panel A worked flat.

Quilted Leaf panel [15 (15, 15, 15, 15, 17, 17, 17, 17) sts]
See also chart, page 58.
Worked in the rnd
Rnd 1: P5 (5, 5, 5, 5, 6, 6, 6, 6), p2tog, yo, k1, yo, ssp, p5 (5, 5, 5, 5, 6, 6, 6, 6).
Rnd 2: P7 (7, 7, 7, 7, 8, 8, 8, 8), k1, p7 (7, 7, 7, 7, 8, 8, 8, 8).
Rnd 3: P4 (4, 4, 4, 4, 5, 5, 5, 5), p2tog, yo, k3, yo, ssp, p4 (4, 4, 4, 4, 5, 5, 5, 5).
Rnd 4: P6 (6, 6, 6, 6, 7, 7, 7, 7), k3, p6 (6, 6, 6, 6, 7, 7, 7, 7).
Rnd 5: P3 (3, 3, 3, 3, 4, 4, 4, 4), p2tog, yo, k5, yo, ssp, p3 (3, 3, 3, 3, 4, 4, 4, 4).
Rnd 6: P5 (5, 5, 5, 5, 6, 6, 6, 6), k5, p5 (5, 5, 5, 5, 6, 6, 6, 6).
Rnd 7: P4 (4, 4, 4, 4, 5, 5, 5, 5), yo, k2, sk2p, k2, yo, p4 (4, 4, 4, 4, 5, 5, 5, 5).
Rnd 8: Rep Rnd 6.
Rnd 9: P5 (5, 5, 5, 5, 6, 6, 6, 6), yo, k1, sk2p, k1, yo, p5 (5, 5, 5, 5, 6, 6, 6, 6).
Rnd 10: Rep Rnd 4.
Rnd 11: P6 (6, 6, 6, 6, 7, 7, 7, 7), yo, sk2p, yo, p6 (6, 6, 6, 6, 7, 7, 7, 7).
Rnd 12: Rep Rnd 2.
Rnds 13-16: Purl.
Repeat Rnds 1-16 for quilted leaf panel in the rnd.

Worked flat
Row 1: (RS) P5 (5, 5, 5, 5, 6, 6, 6, 6), p2tog, yo, k1, yo, ssp, p5 (5, 5, 5, 5, 6, 6, 6, 6).
Row 2: K7 (7, 7, 7, 7, 8, 8, 8, 8), p1, k7 (7, 7, 7, 7, 8, 8, 8, 8).
Row 3: P4 (4, 4, 4, 4, 5, 5, 5, 5), p2tog, yo, k3, yo, ssp, p4 (4, 4, 4, 4, 5, 5, 5, 5).
Row 4: K6 (6, 6, 6, 6, 7, 7, 7, 7), p3, k6 (6, 6, 6, 6, 7, 7, 7, 7).
Row 5: P3 (3, 3, 3, 3, 4, 4, 4, 4), p2tog, yo, k5, yo, ssp, p3 (3, 3, 3, 3, 4, 4, 4, 4).
Row 6: K5 (5, 5, 5, 5, 6, 6, 6, 6), p5, k5 (5, 5, 5, 5, 6, 6, 6, 6).
Row 7: P4 (4, 4, 4, 4, 5, 5, 5, 5), yo, k2, sk2p, k2, yo, p4 (4, 4, 4, 4, 5, 5, 5, 5).
Row 8: Rep Row 6.
Row 9: P5 (5, 5, 5, 5, 6, 6, 6, 6), yo, k1, sk2p, k1, yo, p5 (5, 5, 5, 5, 6, 6, 6, 6).
Row 10: Rep Row 4.
Row 11: P6 (6, 6, 6, 6, 7, 7, 7, 7), yo, sk2p, yo, p6 (6, 6, 6, 6, 7, 7, 7, 7).
Row 12: Rep Row 2.
Row 13: Purl.
Row 14: Knit.
Rows 15 and 16: Rep Rows 13 and 14.
Repeat Rows 1-16 for quilted leaf panel worked flat.

Palm Leaf panel B (begins and ends as 11 sts)
See also chart, page 58.
Worked in the rnd
Rnd 1: Yo, k1, yo, p4, k1, p4, yo, k1, yo—15 sts.
Rnd 2: Yo, k3, yo, p4, k1, p4, yo, k3, yo—19 sts.
Rnd 3: Yo, k5, yo, p4, k1, p4, yo, k5, yo—23 sts.
Rnd 4: Yo, k7, yo, p4, k1, p4, yo, k7, yo—27 sts.
Rnd 5: Yo, k9, yo p4, k1, p4, yo, k9, yo—31 sts.
Rnd 6: Ssk, k7, k2tog, p4, k1, p4, ssk, k7, k2tog—27 sts.
Rnd 7: Ssk, k5, k2tog, p4, k1, p4, ssk, k5, k2tog—23 sts.
Rnd 8: Ssk, k3, k2tog, p4, k1, p4, ssk, k3, k2tog—19 sts.
Rnd 9: Ssk, k1, k2tog, p4, k1, p4, ssk, k1, k2tog—15 sts.
Rnd 10: Sk2p, p4, k1, p4, sk2p —11 sts.
Rnd 11: K1, p4, yo, k1, yo, p4, k1—13 sts.
Rnd 12: K1, p4, yo, k3, yo, p4, k1—15 sts.
Rnd 13: K1, p4, yo, k5, yo, p4, k1—17 sts.
Rnd 14: K1, p4, yo, k7, yo, p4, k1—19 sts.
Rnd 15: K1, p4, yo, k9, yo, p4, k1—21 sts.
Rnd 16: K1, p4, ssk, k7, k2tog, p4, k1—19 sts.
Rnd 17: K1, p4, ssk, k5, k2tog, p4, k1—17 sts.
Rnd 18: K1, p4, ssk, k3, k2tog, p4, k1—15 sts.
Rnd 19: K1, p4, ssk, k1, k2tog, p4, k1—13 sts.
Rnd 20: K1, p4, sk2p, p4, k1—11 sts.
Repeat Rnds 1-20 for palm leaf panel B worked in the rnd.

Worked flat
Row 1: (RS) Yo, k1, yo, p4, k1, p4, yo, k1, yo—15 sts.
Row 2: Yo, p3, yo, k4, p1, k4, yo, p3, yo—19 sts.
Row 3: Yo, k5, yo, p4, k1, p4, yo, k5, yo—23 sts.
Row 4: Yo, p7, yo, k4, p1, k4, yo, p7, yo—27 sts.
Row 5: Yo, k9, yo p4, k1, p4, yo, k9, yo—31 sts.
Row 6: P2tog, p7, ssp, k4, p1, k4, p2tog, p7, ssp—27 sts.
Row 7: Ssk, k5, k2tog, p4, k1, p4, ssk, k5, k2tog—23 sts.
Row 8: P2tog, p3, ssp, k4, p1, k4, p2tog, p3, ssp—19 sts.
Row 9: Ssk, k1, k2tog, p4, k1, p4, ssk, k1, k2tog—15 sts.
Row 10: P3tog-tbl, k4, p1, k4, p3tog-tbl—11 sts.
Row 11: K1, p4, yo, k1, yo, p4, k1—13 sts.

Row 12: P1, k4, yo, p3, yo, k4, p1—15 sts.
Row 13: K1, p4, yo, k5, yo, p4, k1—17 sts.
Row 14: P1, k4, yo, p7, yo, k4, p1—19 sts.
Row 15: K1, p4, yo, k9, yo, p4, k1—21 sts.
Row 16: P1, k4, p2tog, p7, ssp, k4, p1—19 sts.
Row 17: K1, p4, ssk, k5, k2tog, p4, k1—17 sts.
Row 18: P1, k4, p2tog, p3, ssp, k4, p1—15 sts.
Row 19: K1, p4, ssk, k1, k2tog, p4, k1—13 sts.
Row 20: P1, k4, p3tog-tbl, k4, p1—11 sts.
Repeat Rows 1-20 for palm leaf panel B worked flat.

Notes

1. Dress begins at bottom edge of bodice and is worked in the round from waist to underarm. Then back and front are worked flat to the shoulders. Shoulders are shaped with short rows, then joined using the three-needle bind off. At underarm stitches are added at each edge to extend bodice. Sleeve stitches are picked up around the armhole and knitted in the round to the cuff. Neck band is picked up around the neck edge and worked in garter stitch. When the bodice is complete, the skirt is picked up from around the waist and knitted to the bottom edge.
2. Row/round gauge is important in this piece, in order to complete the stitch patterns where they begin and end. The dress is meant to be on the wide and swingy side, so a little wider, or a little narrower, won't affect fit as much as errant row gauge will. The bodice is written in pattern repeat form. To be sure the patterns don't interfere with the neck and shoulder shaping, follow chart precisely and be sure that you are close to row gauge.

3. Stitch patterns are worked in the rnd to underarm. After front and back are separated, the patterns are worked back and forth (flat). Follow stitch pattern instructions (above) for each method.

dress

Bodice

With larger circular needle (circ) and using the long-tail cast on, CO 158 (178, 198, 218, 238, 258, 278, 298, 318) sts. Place marker (pm) for beg of rnd and join to work in the rnd, careful not to twist sts.

Begin panel set up

Rnd 1 *place markers:* *K15 (20, 25, 30, 35, 37, 42, 47, 52), pm, p3 (3, 3, 3, 3, 4, 4, 4, 4), pm, k1, pm, p15 (15, 15, 15, 15, 17, 17, 17, 17), pm, (k1, p4) two times, k1, pm, p15 (15, 15, 15, 15, 17, 17, 17, 17), pm, k1, pm, p3 (3, 3, 3, 3, 4, 4, 4, 4), pm, k15 (20, 25, 30, 35, 37, 42, 47, 52), pm for side; rep from * one more time to end.
Work 3 more rnds as est, slipping markers (sl m).

Begin quilted leaf panels

Next rnd: *Knit to marker (m), sl m, purl to next m, sl m, k1, sl m, work Rnd 1 of quilted leaf to next m, sl m, (k1, p4) two times, k1, sl m, work Rnd 1 of quilted leaf to next m, sl m, k1, sl m, purl to next m, sl m, knit to side m, sl m; rep from * one more time.
Next rnd: *Knit to m, sl m, purl to next m, sl m, k1, sl m, work Rnd 2 of quilted leaf, sl m, (k1, p4) two times, k1, sl m, work Rnd 2 of quilted leaf, sl m, k1, sl m, purl to next m, sl m, knit to side m, sl m; rep from * one more time.

Begin palm leaf panels

Next rnd: *Knit to m, sl m, purl to next m, sl m, work Rnd 1 of palm leaf A to next m, sl m, work Rnd 3 of quilted leaf, work Rnd 1 of palm leaf B to next m, sl m, work Rnd 3 of quilted leaf, work Rnd 1 of palm leaf A to next m, sl m, purl to next m, sl m, knit to side m, sl m; rep from * one more time.

Next rnd: *Knit to m, sl m, purl to next m, sl m, work next rnd of palm leaf A, sl m, work next rnd of quilted leaf, sl m, work next rnd of palm leaf B, sl m, work next rnd of quilted leaf, sl m, work next rnd of palm leaf A, sl m, purl to next m, sl m, knit to side m, sl m; rep from * one more time.

Work 38 (38, 48, 48, 68, 82, 82, 78, 92) more rnds as est, ending after Rnd 20 (20, 10, 10, 10, 4, 4, 20, 14) of palm leaf panels and Rnd 10 (10, 4, 4, 8, 6, 6, 2, 16) of quilted leaf panels.

Pc meas approx 6¼ (6¼, 7½, 7½, 10¼, 12, 12, 11½, 13¼)" [16 (16, 19, 19, 26, 30.5, 30.5, 29, 33.5) cm] from beg.

Begin side shaping

Next rnd *inc rnd:* *K1, M1R, work in est patts to 1 st before side m, M1L, k1, sl m; rep from * one more time (4 sts inc'd)—162 (182, 202, 222, 242, 262, 282, 302, 322) sts.

Next rnd: Work in est patts.

Rep the last two rnds 2 more times—170 (190, 210, 230, 250, 270, 290, 310, 330) sts.

Last rnd worked is Rnd 6 (6, 16, 16, 16, 10, 10, 6, 20) of palm leaf panels and Rnd 16 (16, 10, 10, 14, 12, 12, 8, 6) of quilted leaf panels.

Separate front and back

Next row: Using the cable cast on, CO 6 sts, knit to m, sl m, purl to next m, sl m, work next RS of each panel, sl m, purl to next m, sl m, knit to side m, then place rem sts for back onto waste yarn. Place locking stitch marker on this row on the front for ease in counting rows to shoulder when working back.

Front

Next row: (WS) Using the cable cast on, CO 6 sts, purl to m, sl m, knit to next m, sl m, work next WS row of each panel, sl m, knit to next m, sl m, purl to end—97 (107, 117, 127, 137, 147, 157, 167, 177) sts on needle.

Next row: (RS) Work St st and panels as est to end.

Work 41 (41, 51, 51, 47, 49, 49, 53, 67) more rows even, ending after Row 10 (10, 10, 10, 6, 2, 2, 2, 10) of palm leaf panels and Row 12 (12, 16, 16, 16, 16, 16, 16, 12) of quilted leaf panels.

Sizes 33¼ (37½, 41¾, 46, -, -, -, -, 67)" [84.5 (95.5, 106, 117, -, -, -, -, 170) cm] only:
Proceed to All sizes.

Sizes - (-, -, -, 50, 54¼, 58½, 62¾, -)" [- (-, -, -, 127, 138, 148.5, 159.5, -) cm] only:
Note: Quilted leaf panels end here to avoid a partial repeat at neck edge. Work quilted leaf panel sts in reverse stockinette to end of neck shaping.

Next row: (RS) Knit to m, sl m, purl to next m, sl m, work next row of palm leaf A, sl m, purl to next m, sl m, work next row of palm leaf B, sl m, purl to next m, sl m, work next row of palm leaf A, sl m, purl to next m, knit to end.

Work - (-, -, -, 3, 7, 7, 7, -) more rows as est.

All sizes

Last row worked is Row 10 of palm leaf panels.
Pc meas approx 5¾ (5¾, 7¼, 7¼, 7¼, 8, 8, 8½, 9¼)" [14.5 (14.5, 18.5, 18.5, 18.5, 20.5, 20.5, 21.5, 23.5) cm] from underarm.

Begin neck and shoulder shaping

Note: Do not count yarnovers as stitches.

Next row *short row 1:* (RS) Knit to m, sl m, purl to next m, sl m, work palm leaf A, sl m, purl to next m, remove m, p1, join a new ball of yarn and BO 9 sts to next m, removing m to BO last st, purl to next m, sl m, work palm leaf A, sl m, purl to next m, knit to last 4 (4, 4, 5, 5, 5, 6, 6, 7) sts, turn—44 (49, 54, 59, 64, 69, 74, 79, 84) sts rem for each side; (WS) yo, purl to m, sl m, knit to next m, sl m, work palm leaf A, sl m, knit to left neck edge; on right neck edge, BO 4 (4, 4, 4, 4, 5, 5, 5, 5) sts, knit to m, work palm leaf A, sl m, knit to next m, sl m, purl to last 4 (4, 4, 5, 5, 5, 6, 6, 7) sts, turn.

Next row *short row 2:* (RS) Yo, work in est patts to neck edge; then BO 4 (4, 4, 4, 4, 5, 5, 5, 5) sts, work in est patts to 3 (3, 4, 4, 5, 5, 6, 6, 7) sts before last gap, turn—40 (45, 50, 55, 60, 64, 69, 74, 79) sts rem each side; (WS) yo, work in est patts to neck edge; then BO 3 (3, 3, 3, 3, 4, 4, 4, 4) sts, work in est patts to 3 (3, 4, 4, 5, 5, 6, 6, 7) sts before last gap, turn.

Next row *short row 3:* (RS) Yo, work to neck edge; then BO 3 (3, 3, 3, 3, 4, 4, 4, 4) sts, work to 3 (3, 4, 4, 5, 5, 6, 6, 7) sts before last gap, turn—37 (42, 47, 52, 57, 60, 65, 70, 75) sts rem each side; (WS) yo, work to neck edge; then BO 2 sts, work to last 3 (3, 4, 4, 5, 5, 6, 6, 7) sts, turn.

Next row *short row 4:* (RS) Yo, work to neck edge; then BO 2 sts, work to 3 (3, 4, 4, 5, 5, 6, 6, 7) sts before last gap, turn—35 (40, 45, 50, 55, 58, 63, 68, 73) sts rem each side; (WS) yo, work to neck edge; then work to 3 (3, 4, 4, 5, 5, 6, 6, 7) sts before last gap, turn.

Next row *short row 5:* (RS) Yo, work to 2 sts before neck edge, ssk; then k2tog, work to 3 (3, 4, 4, 5, 5, 5, 6, 6) sts before last gap, turn—34 (39, 44, 49, 54, 57, 62, 67, 72) sts rem each side; (WS) yo, work to neck edge; then work to 3 (3, 4, 4, 5, 5, 5, 6, 6) sts before last gap, turn.
Rep *short row five* 0 (3, 1, 3, 1, 3, 1, 3, 3) time(s)—34 (36, 43, 46, 53, 54, 61, 64, 69) sts rem each side.

Next row *short row 6:* (RS) Yo, work to 2 sts before neck edge, ssk; then k2tog, work to 2 (3, 3, 4, 4, 5, 5, 6, 6) sts before last gap, turn—33 (35, 42, 45, 52, 53, 60, 63, 68) sts rem each side; (WS) yo, work to neck edge; then work to 2 (3, 3, 4, 4, 5, 5, 6, 6) sts before last gap, turn.
Rep *short row six* 3 (0, 2, 0, 2, 0, 2, 0, 0) more times—30 (35, 40, 45, 50, 53, 58, 63, 68) sts rem each side.

Next row *short row 7:* (RS) Yo, work to neck edge; then work to 2 (3, 3, 4, 4, 4, 5, 5, 6) sts before last gap, turn; (WS) yo, work to neck edge; then work to 2 (3, 3, 4, 4, 4, 5, 5, 6) sts before last gap, turn.

Resolve short rows

Next row: (RS) Yo, work in patts to neck edge; then work in patts to first yo, p2tog the yo with the st after gap, then knit to end, working k2tog to join each yo with the st after gap. Break yarn at right armhole edge.

Next row: (WS) On left neck edge, work in patts to first yo, ssk the yo with the st after gap, then purl to end, working ssp to join each yo with the st after gap.
Break yarn.

Back

Return sts held for back to larger circ.
Next row: (RS) With RS of back facing and beg at right armhole edge, pick up and knit 6 sts in underarm CO from right front, knit to m, sl m, purl to next m, sl m, work Row 7 (7, 17, 17, 17, 11, 11, 7, 1) of palm leaf A, sl m, work Row 1 (1, 11, 11, 15, 13, 13, 9, 7) of quilted leaf, sl m, work Row 7 (7, 17, 17, 17, 11, 11, 7, 1) of palm leaf B, sl m, work Row 1 (1, 11, 11, 15, 13, 13, 9, 7) of quilted leaf, sl m, work Row 7 (7, 17, 17, 17, 11, 11, 7, 1) of palm leaf A, sl m, purl to next m, sl m, knit to end, then pick up and knit 6 sts in underarm CO from left front—97 (107, 117, 127, 137, 147, 157, 167, 177) sts on needle. Place locking stitch marker on this row for counting.
Next row: (WS) Work St st and panels as est to end.
Work 42 (42, 52, 52, 52, 58, 58, 62, 68) more rows even, ending after Row 10 of palm leaf panels and Row 12 (12, 16, 16, 4, 8, 8, 8, 12) of quilted leaf panels. Place a locking st marker on either side of center 37 (37, 37, 37, 37, 41, 41, 41, 41) sts for neck.

Begin shoulder shaping

Note: **For sizes - (-, 41¾, 46, 50, -, -, -, -)" [- (-, 106, 117, 127, -, -, -, -) cm] only:** to avoid a partial repeat of quilted leaf panels, after completing the next repeat of quilted leaf, continue working those sts in reverse stockinette.
Do not count yarnovers as stitches.
Next row *short row 1:* (RS) Work in est patts to last 4 (4, 4, 5, 5, 5, 6, 6, 7) sts, turn; (WS) yo, work in est patts to last 4 (4, 4, 5, 5, 5, 6, 6, 7) sts, turn.

Next row *short row 2:* (RS) Yo, work to 3 (3, 4, 4, 5, 5, 6, 6, 7) sts before last gap, turn; (WS) yo, work to 3 (3, 4, 4, 5, 5, 6, 6, 7) sts before last gap.
Rep *short row two* 3 (7, 4, 7, 4, 7, 2, 7, 2) more times.

Next row *short row 3:* (RS) Yo, work to 2 (3, 3, 4, 4, 4, 5, 5, 6) sts before last gap, turn; (WS) yo, work to 2 (3, 3, 4, 4, 4, 5, 5, 6) sts before last gap.
Rep *short row three* 4 (0, 3, 0, 3, 0, 5, 0, 5) more times.
Last row worked is Row 10 of palm leaf panels.

Resolve short rows

Next row: (RS) Yo, work to neck m, remove m, BO all sts to next neck m, removing marker to BO last st, work in patts to first yo, p2tog the yo with the st after the gap, then knit to end, working k2tog to join each yo with the st after gap.
Break yarn, leaving a tail roughly five times the width of the shoulder for finishing. Join yarn at right neck edge, ready to work a WS row.

Next row: (WS) Work to first yo, ssk the yo with the st after the gap, then purl to end, working ssp to join each yo with the st after gap.
Do not break yarn.

Join shoulders
Place sts held for front shoulders to spare circ. With RS of pcs held tog and attached yarn, using the three-needle bind off, BO all left shoulder sts. With long tail at right armhole edge, rep for right shoulder.

Gently steam block piece, keeping marker in CO edge in place.

Sleeves
With RS facing and larger double-pointed needles (dpns), beg at underarm, pick up and knit 38 (38, 45, 45, 45, 50, 50, 54, 60) sts along armhole edge to shoulder seam (approx 4 sts for every 5 rows), then pick up and knit 38 (38, 45, 45, 45, 50, 50, 54, 60) sts to underarm—76 (76, 90, 90, 90, 100, 100, 108, 120) sts on needles. Pm for BOR.
First rnd: Knit.
Cont in St st until sleeve meas 17½ (17½, 17½, 17½, 17, 17, 17, 16½, 16½)" [44.5 (44.5, 44.5, 44.5, 43, 43, 43, 42, 42) cm] from pick-up.
Change to smaller dpns.

Begin gathered cuff
Sizes 33¼ (37½, -, -, -, -, -, -, -)" [84.5 (95.5, -, -, -, -, -, -, -) cm] only:
Proceed to All sizes.

Sizes - (-, 41¾, 46, 50, 54¼, 58½, 62¾, 67)" [- (-, 106, 117, 127, 138, 148.5, 159.5, 170) cm] only:
Next rnd *dec rnd:* *K- (-, 7, 7, 7, 3, 8, 4, 2), k2tog; rep from * to end; - (-, 10, 10, 10, 20, 10, 18, 30) sts dec'd— - (-, 80, 80, 80, 80, 90, 90, 90) sts rem.

All sizes
Next rnd *dec rnd:* *K2tog; rep from * to end—38 (38, 40, 40, 40, 40, 45, 45, 45) sts rem.
Next rnd: Purl.
Next rnd: Knit.
Rep the last 2 rnds two more times.
Next rnd: Bind off purlwise.

Neck band
With RS facing and smaller, shorter circ, beg at right shoulder seam, pick up and knit 1 st in each BO st and 1 stitch in each row around neck edge. Pm for BOR.
First rnd: Purl.
Next rnd: Knit.
Rep the last 2 rnds two more times.
Next rnd: Bind off purlwise.

Skirt
With RS facing, larger, longer circ and beg at tail from bodice cast on (side edge), pick up and knit 1 st in each CO st and increase as follows: *pick up and knit 1 st, m1-L/loop; rep from * to end—316 (356, 396, 436, 476, 516, 556, 596, 636) sts on needle. Pm for BOR.

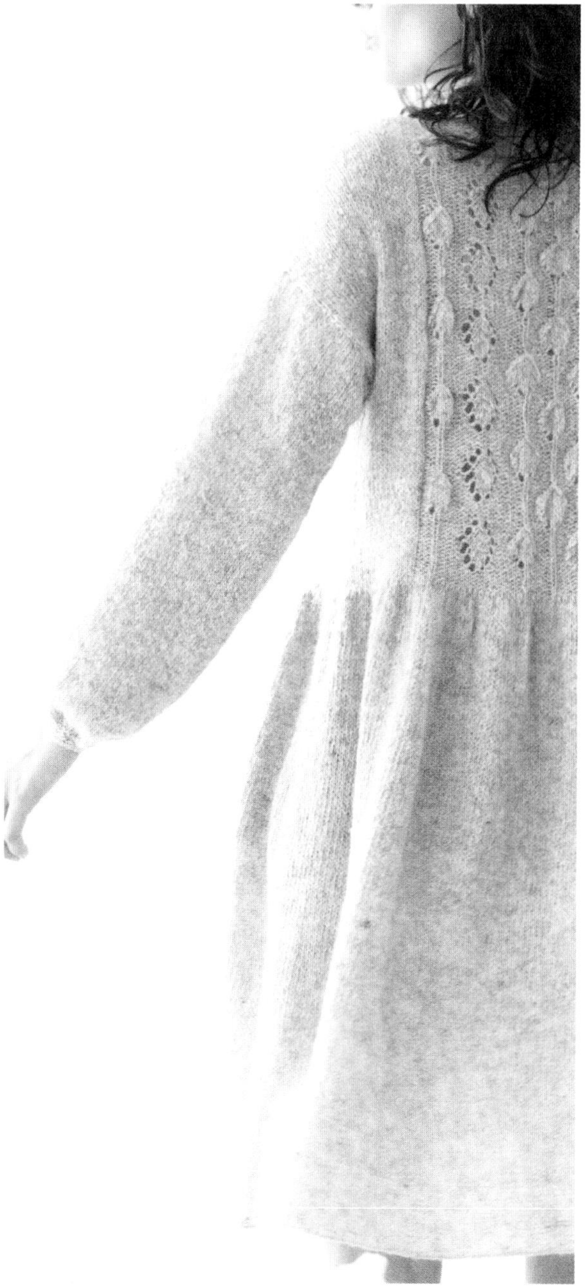

Begin stockinette
First rnd: Knit.
Knit 10 more rnds.
Next rnd *place marker:* K158 (178, 198, 218, 238, 258, 278, 298, 318), pm for side, k158 (178, 198, 218, 238, 258, 278, 298, 318) sts to end.

Begin side shaping
Next rnd *inc rnd:* *K1, M1L, knit to 1 st before m, M1R, k1, sl m; rep from * one more time (4 sts inc'd)—320 (360, 400, 440, 480, 520, 560, 600, 640) sts.
Rep *inc rnd* every 12 rnds eight more times—352 (392, 432, 472, 512, 552, 592, 632, 672) sts.
Knit 3 rnds.
Skirt meas approx 15" [38 cm] from pick-up.

Begin reverse stockinette
Next rnd: Purl.
Purl 2 more rnds.
Next rnd *inc rnd:* *P1, m1-p/L, purl to 1 st before m, m1-p/R, p1; rep from * one more time (4 sts inc'd)—356 (396, 436, 476, 516, 556, 596, 636, 676) sts.
Rep *inc rnd* every 12 rnds one more time—360 (400, 440, 480, 520, 560, 600, 640, 680) sts.
Cont in rev St st until skirt meas 21" [53.5 cm] from pick-up.
Next rnd: Bind off all sts purlwise.

Finishing
Weave in ends. Steam lightly.

Palm Leaf panel A

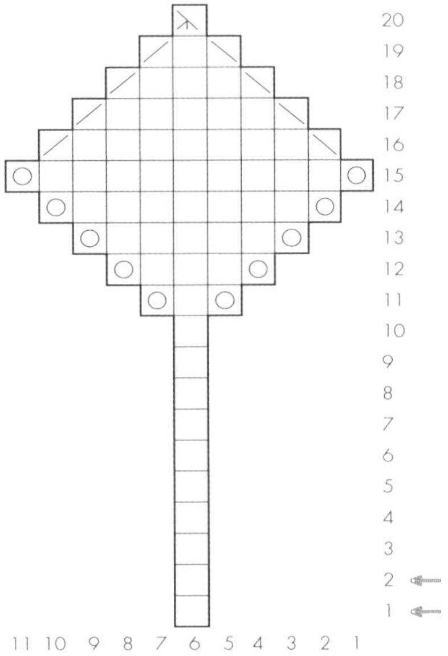

Quilted Leaf panel

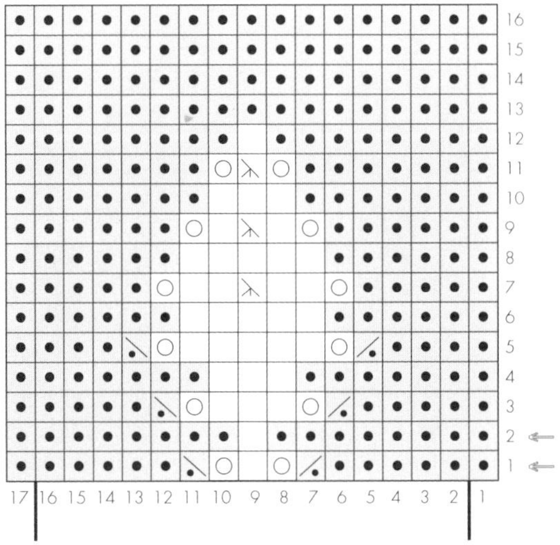

Note: When working flat, read even-numbered rows from left to right.

Palm Leaf panel B

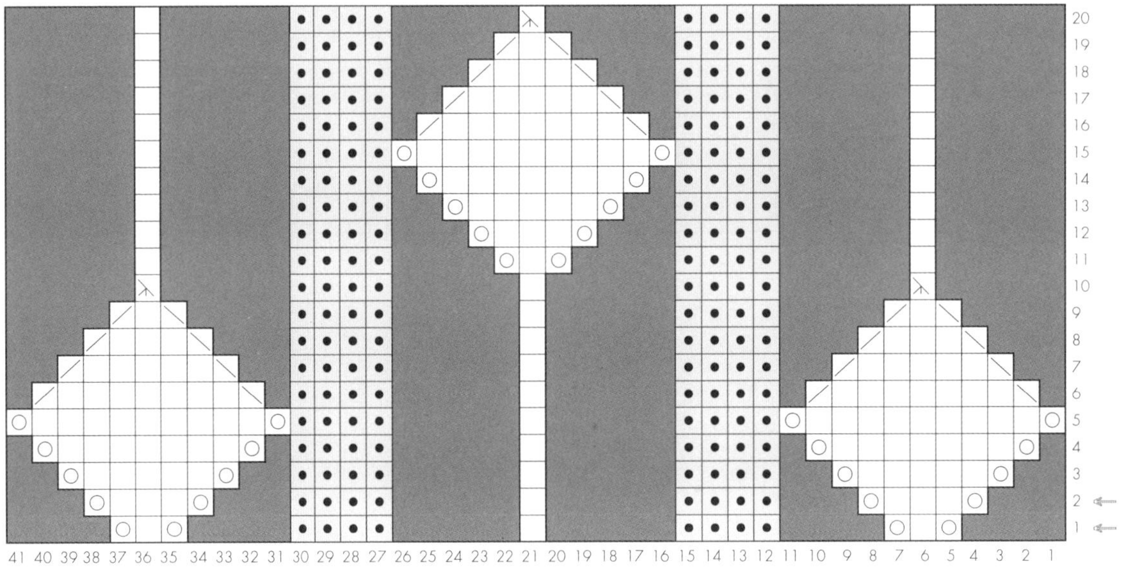

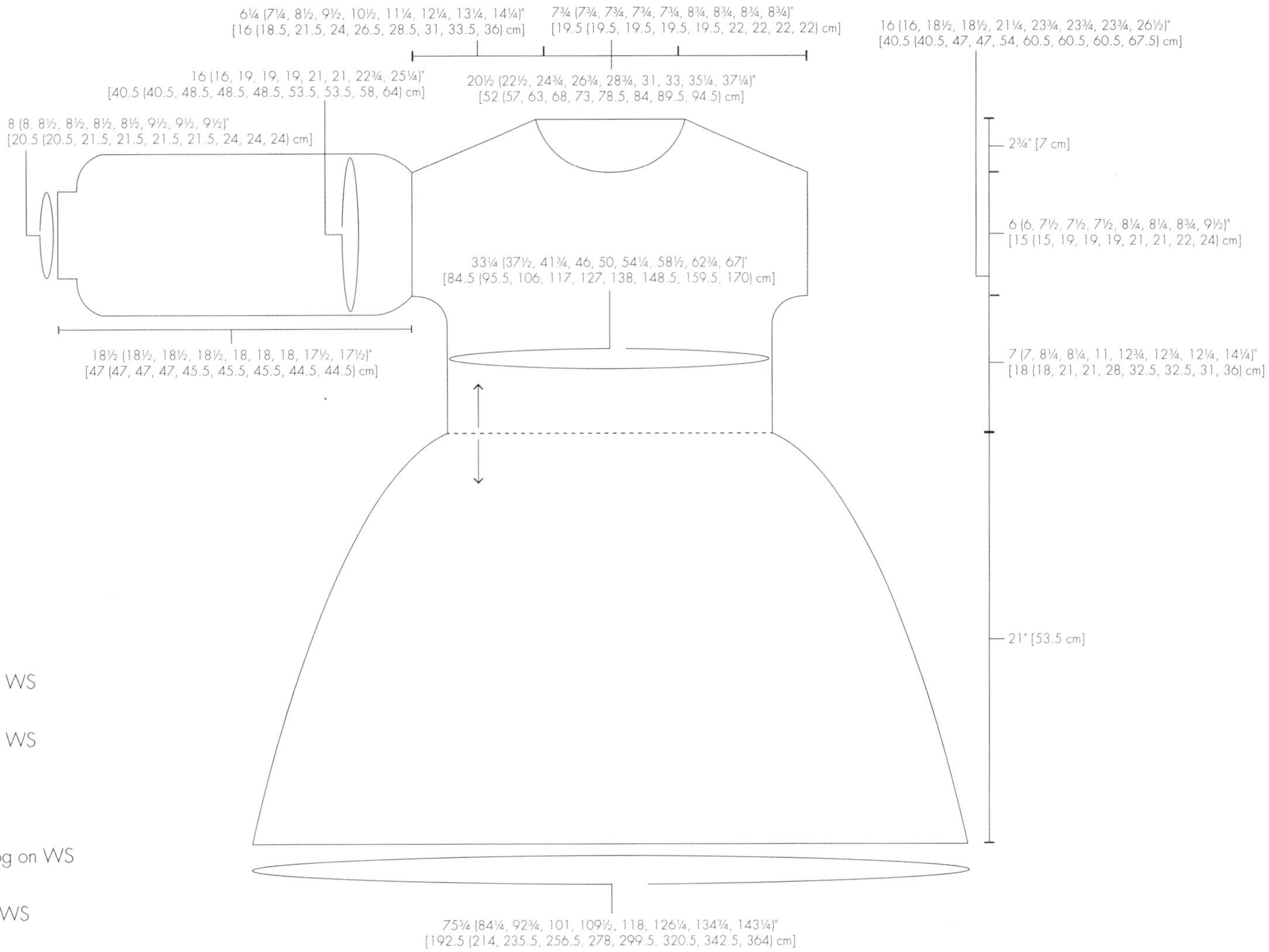

Key

- knit on RS, purl on WS
- purl on RS, knit on WS
- yo
- k2tog on RS, p2tog on WS
- ssk on RS, ssp on WS
- sk2p on RS, p3tog-tbl on WS
- ssp on RS
- p2tog on RS
- no stitch

bayberry

The yoke pattern on Bayberry is a rare instance of things coming together on a first try. The palette and blocky color pattern, which incorporates both knit and purl stitches, couldn't be simpler. The use of purl bumps in a different color on an otherwise stockinette ground creates small highlights of contrast. In this instance, Owl's tweedy texture and heathered colors add still another layer of texture and color play. The shape of this sweater is overtly cocoon-like: The yoke is extra-long (more room for color patterning) and the hem tapers in a bit, folding you in like closing wings.

Finished measurements
44 (48½, 53, 57½, 62, 66½, 71, 75½)" [112 (123, 134.5, 146, 157.5, 169, 180.5, 192) cm] bust circumference; shown in size 53" [134.5 cm] on a 31" [79 cm], 5'11" [180 cm] tall model (22" [56 cm] positive ease)

Yarn
Owl by Quince & Co
(50% American wool, 50% alpaca; 120yd [110m]/50g)
- 6 (7, 7, 8, 9, 10, 11, 12) skeins Elf 303 (A)
- 1 (1, 1, 1, 2, 2, 2, 2) skeins Sokoke 304 (B)
- 1 skein Taiga 328 (C)
- 1 skein Lagoon 330 (D)
- 1 skein Yucca 317(E)
- 1 skein Straits 329 (F)

Needles
- One 16" circular needle (circ) in size US 8 [5 mm]
- One 32" circ in size US 8 [5 mm]
- One 16" circ in size US 10 [6 mm]
- One 32" circ in size US 10 [6 mm]
- One set double-pointed needles (dpns) in size US 10 [6 mm]

Or size to obtain gauge

Notions
- Stitch markers
- Waste yarn
- Tapestry needle

Gauge
16 sts and 24 rnds = 4" [10 cm] in stockinette stitch with larger needle, after light steam blocking.

Notes
1. Body is knitted in the round from the bottom up to underarm. Stitches are held for underarm, then more stitches are cast on for sleeves using waste yarn. Round yoke is continued in color/stitch patterns to neck edge. Sleeve stitches are picked up from waste yarn cast on and knitted in the round to the cuff.
2. When picking up live stitches from the bottom edge of cast on, you will have one more stitch than the number you cast on. See page 114 for an illustrated tutorial.

This pattern requires five different colors. If you'd like to use them up, consider working them into the Snowberry Hat at the end of this book. Or use the basic pattern for your own arrangement of stripes.

pullover

With A, smaller, longer circular needle (circ), and using the long-tail cast on, CO 180 (202, 224, 246, 268, 290, 312, 334) sts. Place marker (pm) for beg of rnd (BOR) and join to work in the rnd, careful not to twist sts.

Begin ribbed border
First rnd: *K1, p1; rep from * to end.
Cont in est rib for 1" [2.5 cm].
Change to larger circ.

Begin stockinette stitch
Next rnd *dec rnd*: K4, *ssk, k3, k2tog, k4, k2tog, k3, ssk, k4; rep from * to end; 32 (36, 40, 44, 48, 52, 56, 60) sts dec'd—148 (166, 184, 202, 220, 238, 256, 274) sts rem.
Next row *place marker*: K74 (83, 92, 101, 110, 119, 128, 137), pm for side, k74 (83, 92, 101, 110, 119, 128, 137) sts to end (BOR counts as second side marker).
Next 2 rnds: Knit.
Next rnd *inc rnd*: *K2, M1L, knit to 2 sts before side m, M1R, k2, sl m; rep from * one more time (4 sts inc'd)—152 (170, 188, 206, 224, 242, 260, 278) sts.
Rep *inc rnd* every 6 (6, 6, 7, 7, 7, 8, 8) rnds six more times—176 (194, 212, 230, 248, 266, 284, 302) sts.
Cont in St st until pc meas 10 (10, 10, 11, 11, 11, 12, 12)" [25.5 (25.5, 25.5, 28, 28, 28, 30.5, 30.5) cm] from beg.

Separate front and back
Next rnd: *Knit to side m, remove m, k7, then place the 14 sts just worked onto waste yarn; rep from * one more time—74 (83, 92, 101, 110, 119, 128, 137) sts rem each for front and back.

Begin yoke
Next rnd: Knit across back sts, turn work, with waste yarn, make a slipknot (first sleeve st), place onto RH needle, using the backward loop cast on, CO 23 (27, 31, 35, 39, 43, 47, 51) more sts for sleeve, turn work, pm for raglan, with A, knit across CO sts, pm for raglan, knit across front sts, turn work, with waste yarn, make slipknot (first sleeve st), place onto RH needle, using the backward loop cast on, CO 23 (27, 31, 35, 39, 43, 47, 51) more sts for sleeve, turn work, pm for raglan, with A, knit across CO sts, pm for raglan—196 (222, 248, 274, 300, 326, 352, 378) sts on needle. Break yarn. Sl next 37 (42, 46, 51, 55, 60, 64, 69) sts to RH needle, pm for BOR. Rejoin yarn.
Next 2 rnds: Knit.

Begin yoke shaping
Next rnd *dec rnd*: *Knit to 2 sts before m, ssk, sl m, knit to next m, sl m, k2tog; rep from * one more time, knit to end (4 sts dec'd)—192 (218, 244, 270, 296, 322, 348, 374) rem.
Rep *dec rnd* every rnd 3 (5, 7, 9, 11, 13, 15, 17) more times—180 (198, 216, 234, 252, 270, 288, 306) sts rem. Pc meas 1¼ (1½, 1¾, 2¼, 2½, 2¾, 3¼, 3½)" [3 (4, 4.5, 5.5, 6.5, 7, 8.5, 9) cm] from sleeve cast on.

Begin colorwork pattern and round yoke shaping
Next rnd: Work Rnd 1 of Chart 1, removing raglan markers.
Work Rnds 2-5 of Chart 1.
Next rnd *dec rnd*: With A, k3, k2tog, *k7, k2tog; rep from * to last 4 sts, k4; 20 (22, 24, 26, 28, 30, 32, 34) sts dec'd—160 (176, 192, 208, 224, 240, 256, 272) sts rem.

Continue colorwork
Next rnd: Work Rnd 1 of Chart 2.
Work Rnds 2-7 of Chart 2.

Sizes - (48½, -, 57½, -, 66½, -, 75½)" [- (123, -, 146, -, 169, -, 192) cm] only:
Next rnd: With B, knit.
Proceed to All sizes.

Sizes 44 (-, 53, -, 62, -, 71, -)" [112 (-, 134.5, -, 157.5, -, 180.5, -) cm] only:
Next rnd *dec rnd*: With B, k2, k2tog, *k6, k2tog; rep from * to last 4 sts, k4; 20 (-, 24, -, 28, -, 32, -) sts dec'd—140 (-, 168, -, 196, -, 224, -) sts rem.

All sizes
Continue colorwork
Note: Change to shorter, larger circ when necessary.
Next rnd: Work Rnd 1 of Chart 3.
Work Rnds 2-10 of Chart 3.
Next rnd *dec rnd*: With A, k1, k2tog, *k5 (2, 5, 2, 5, 2, 5, 2), k2tog; rep from * to last 4 (1, 4, 1, 4, 1, 4, 1) st(s), k4 (1, 4, 1, 4, 1, 4, 1); 20 (44, 24, 52, 28, 60, 32, 68) sts dec'd—120 (132, 144, 156, 168, 180, 192, 204) sts rem.

Continue colorwork
Next rnd: Work Rnd 1 of Chart 4.
Work Rnds 2-12 of Chart 4.

Sizes - (48½, -, 57½, -, 66½, -, 75½)" [- (123, -, 146, -, 169, -, 192) cm] only:
Next rnd: With B, knit.
Proceed to All sizes.

Sizes 44 (-, 53, -, 62, -, 71, -)" [112 (-, 134.5, -, 157.5, -, 180.5, -) cm] only:
Next rnd *dec rnd*: With B, k2, k2tog, *k4, k2tog; rep from * to last 2 sts, k2; 20 (-, 24, -, 28, -, 32, -) sts dec'd—100 (-, 120, -, 140, -, 160, -) sts rem.

All sizes
Continue colorwork
Next rnd: Work Rnd 1 of Chart 5.
Work Rnds 2-11 of Chart 5.
Next rnd *dec rnd*: With B, k1, k2tog, *k3 (1, 3, 1, 3, 1, 3, 1), k2tog; rep from * to last 2 (0, 2, 0, 2, 0, 2, 0) sts, k2 (0, 2, 0, 2, 0, 2, 0); 20 (44, 24, 52, 28, 60, 32, 68) sts dec'd—80 (88, 96, 104, 112, 120, 128, 136) sts rem.

Continue colorwork
Next rnd: Work Rnd 1 of Chart 6.
Work Rnds 2-8 of Chart 6. Break all colors except A.
Next rnd *dec rnd*: *K2tog, k2; rep from * to end; 20 (22, 24, 26, 28, 30, 32, 34) sts dec'd—60 (66, 72, 78, 84, 90, 96, 102) sts rem.

Begin short row back neck shaping
Note: Do not count yarnovers as stitches.
Next row *short row 1*: (RS) K24 (27, 30, 33, 36, 39, 42, 45), turn; (WS) yo, p48 (54, 60, 66, 72, 78, 84, 90), turn.

Next row *short row 2*: (RS) Yo, knit to 4 (5, 6, 7, 8, 9, 10, 11) sts before last gap, turn; (WS) yo, purl to 4 (5, 6, 7, 8, 9, 10, 11) sts before last gap, turn.
Rep *short row 2* two more times.

Resolve short rows and begin neck band
Next row: (RS) Yo, knit to BOR.
Change to smaller, shorter circ.
Next rnd: *K1, p1; rep from * to end, working k2tog or ssp in pattern to join each yarnover with the st after gap.
Cont in rib for 2 more rnds.
Next rnd: Bind off in pattern.

Sleeves
With A, RS facing, and larger double-pointed needles (dpns), place first 7 sts held for underarm onto needle, pm for BOR, place rem 7 underarm sts onto needle, then working one st at a time, pick out waste yarn from sleeve cast on and place each st onto needle, sl 7 underarm sts to RH needle—39 (43, 47, 51, 55, 59, 63, 67) sts on needles.
First rnd: K6, k2tog (picked up st and last held st), knit to last 8 sts, ssk, k6 (2 sts dec'd)—37 (41, 45, 49, 53, 57, 61, 65) sts rem.
Next rnd: Knit.
Cont in St st until pc meas 1" [2.5 cm] from underarm.

Begin sleeve shaping
Next rnd *dec rnd*: K2, k2tog, knit to last 4 sts, ssk, k2 (2 sts dec'd)—35 (39, 43, 47, 51, 55, 59, 63) sts rem.
Rep *dec rnd* every 12 (8, 8, 6, 6, 4, 4, 4) rnds 2 (3, 3, 4, 4, 6, 6, 6) more times—31 (33, 37, 39, 43, 43, 47, 51) sts.
Cont in St st until sleeve meas 7" [18 cm] from underarm.
Next rnd *inc rnd*: K1 (0, 1, 3, 3, 3, 2, 1), [M1L, k10 (11, 12, 12, 8, 8, 9, 10)] to end; 3 (3, 3, 3, 5, 5, 5, 5) sts inc'd—34 (36, 40, 42, 48, 48, 52, 56) sts.

Begin ribbed cuff
Next rnd: *K1, p1; rep from * to end.
Cont in est rib for 7" [18 cm].
Next rnd: Bind off in pattern.

Finishing
Weave in ends. Steam gently.

Chart 1

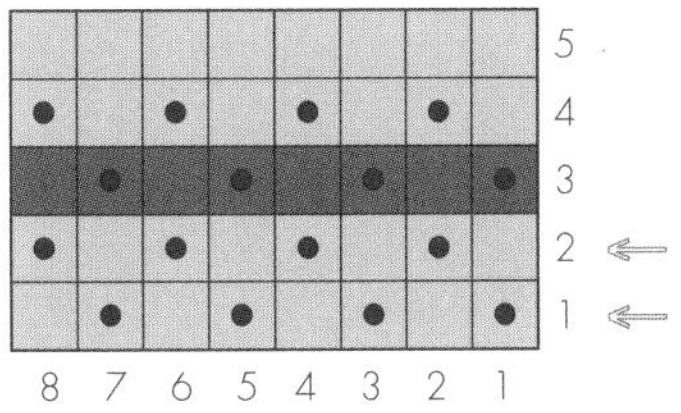

Chart 2

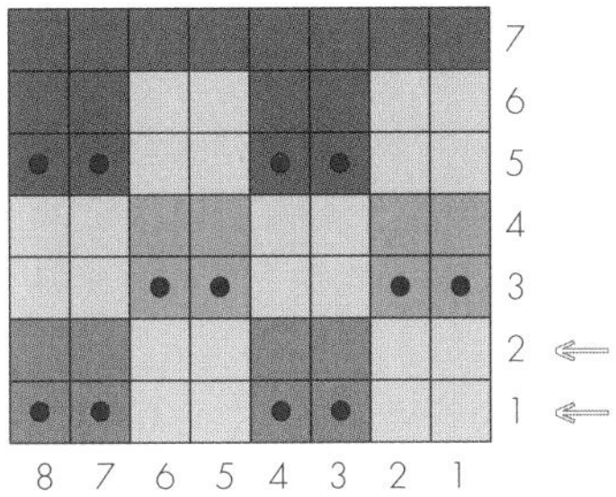

Key

- knit in specified color
- • purl in specified color
- with A, work as specified
- with B, work as specified
- with C, work as specified
- with D, work as specified
- with E, work as specified
- with F, work as specified

Chart 5

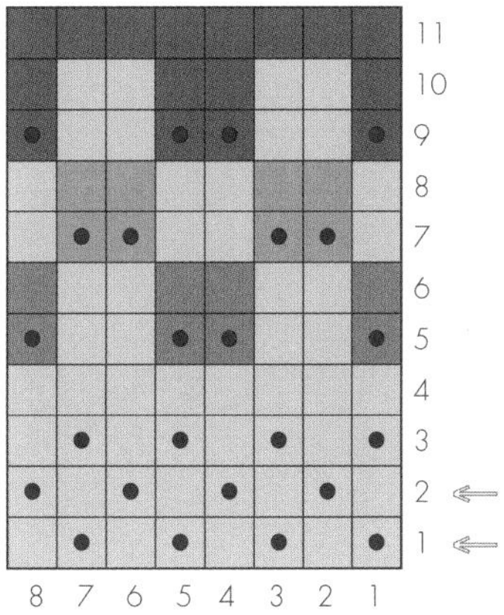

Chart 3

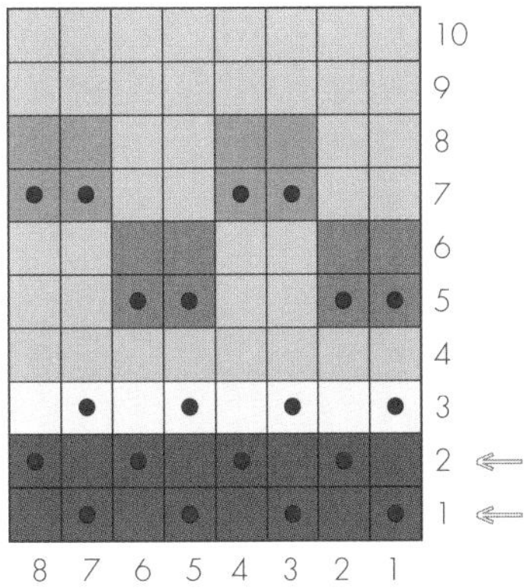

Chart 4

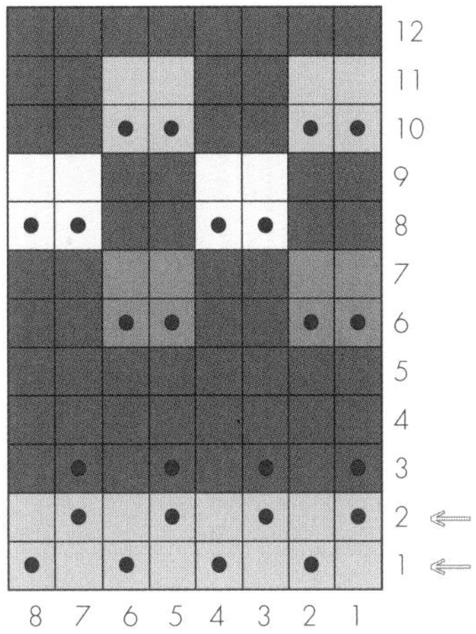

Chart 6

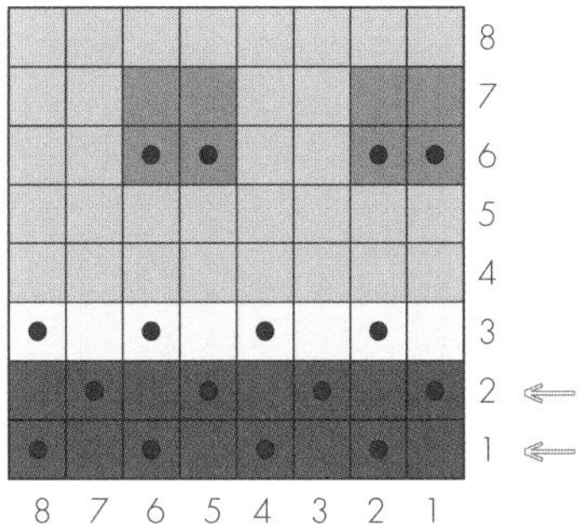

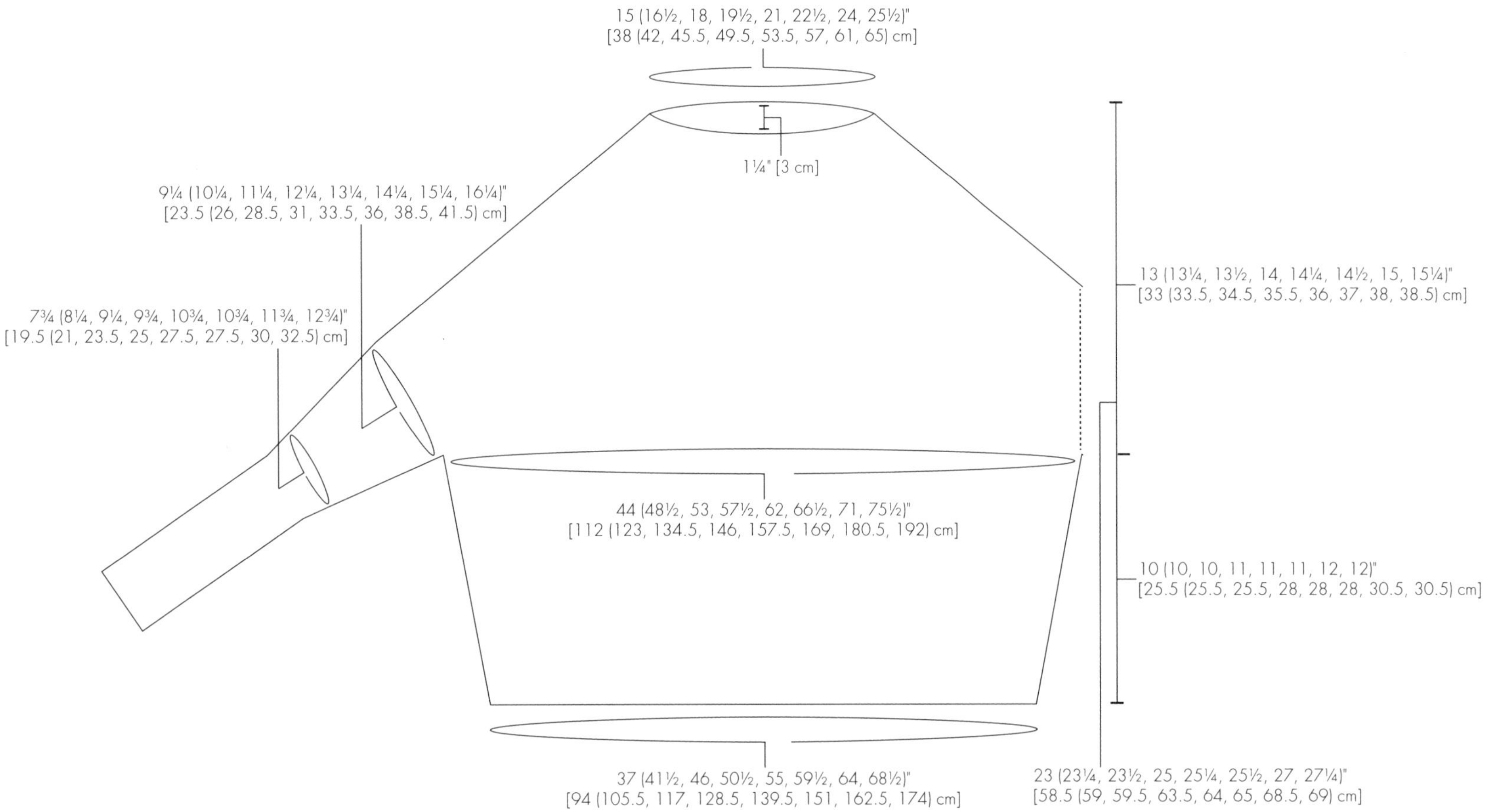
15 (16½, 18, 19½, 21, 22½, 24, 25½)"
[38 (42, 45.5, 49.5, 53.5, 57, 61, 65) cm]
1¼" [3 cm]
9¼ (10¼, 11¼, 12¼, 13¼, 14¼, 15¼, 16¼)"
[23.5 (26, 28.5, 31, 33.5, 36, 38.5, 41.5) cm]
7¾ (8¼, 9¼, 9¾, 10¾, 10¾, 11¾, 12¾)"
[19.5 (21, 23.5, 25, 27.5, 27.5, 30, 32.5) cm]
13 (13¼, 13½, 14, 14¼, 14½, 15, 15¼)"
[33 (33.5, 34.5, 35.5, 36, 37, 38, 38.5) cm]
44 (48½, 53, 57½, 62, 66½, 71, 75½)"
[112 (123, 134.5, 146, 157.5, 169, 180.5, 192) cm]
10 (10, 10, 11, 11, 11, 12, 12)"
[25.5 (25.5, 25.5, 28, 28, 28, 30.5, 30.5) cm]
37 (41½, 46, 50½, 55, 59½, 64, 68½)"
[94 (105.5, 117, 128.5, 139.5, 151, 162.5, 174) cm]
23 (23¼, 23½, 25, 25¼, 25½, 27, 27¼)"
[58.5 (59, 59.5, 63.5, 64, 65, 68.5, 69) cm]

elderberry

A populated cable sweater has never been my favorite thing. It's not at all that I don't love the way they look, those traditional, cream-colored Aran sweaters, those modern cable patterns that twine dramatically in and around. But wearing them—not so keen. They often feel like a suit of armor—stiffer than I like and heavy. So, for this pullover, I pushed the needle size up and up to see if I could get a more forgiving fabric, something lighter and more responsive. And it worked!

Finished measurements
40½ (44½, 47½, 51½, 55½, 59½, 62½, 66½, 70½, 74½)" [103 (113, 120.5, 131, 141, 151, 159, 169, 179, 189) cm] bust circumference; shown in size 47½" [120.5 cm] on a 31" [79 cm], 5'11" [180 cm] tall model (16½" [42 cm] positive ease)

Yarn
Owl by Quince & Co
(50% American wool, 50% alpaca; 120yd [110m]/50g)
- 9 (10, 10, 11, 12, 13, 14, 15, 16, 17) skeins Albertine 306

Needles
- One 32" circular needle (circ) in size US 7 [4.5 mm]
- One 16" circ in size US 8 [5 mm]
- One 32" circ in size US 10½ [6.5 mm]
- One set double-pointed needles in size US 10½ [6.5 mm]

Or size to obtain gauge

Notions
- Stitch markers
- Locking stitch markers
- Cable needle (optional)
- Waste yarn
- Tapestry needle

Gauge
- 16 sts and 24 rnds = 4" [10 cm] in texture pattern with largest needle, after light steam blocking
- 21½ sts and 24 rnds = 4" [10 cm] in center cable with largest needle, after light steam blocking
- Each side panel = 6½" [16.5 cm] wide.

Texture pattern for swatching (even number of stitches)
See also chart, page 70.
Worked in the rnd
Rnd 1: *P1, k1; rep from * to end.
Rnd 2: Purl.
Repeat Rnds 1 and 2 for texture pattern for swatching.

Right side panel (35 stitches)
See also chart, page 70.
Worked in the rnd
Rnd 1: P2, k13, p1, RT, k1, p1, k13, p2.
Rnd 2: P2, k13, p1, k3, p1, k13, p2.
Rnd 3: P2, C6B, k1, C6F, p1, k1, LT, p1, C6B, k1, C6F, p2.
Rnd 4: Rep Rnd 2.
Repeat Rnds 1-4 for right side panel in the rnd.

Worked flat
Row 1: (RS) P2, k13, p1, RT, k1, p1, k13, p2.
Row 2: K2, p13, k1, p3, k1, p13, k2.
Row 3: P2, C6B, k1, C6F, p1, k1, LT, p1, C6B, k1, C6F, p2.
Row 4: Rep Row 2.
Repeat Rows 1-4 for right side panel worked flat.

> I like a sweater that hangs straight, rather than gathering in at the hem. But finding the right number of stitches to increase or decrease at the transition of rib to body patterns is always a challenge. If you find your ribbed border to be too loose or pulling in more than you'd like, readjust the number of stitches to add or subtract. You're in charge. Yes, really.

Left side panel (35 stitches)
See also chart, page 70.
Worked in the rnd
Rnd 1: P2, k13, p1, k1, LT, p1, k13, p2.
Rnd 2: P2, k13, p1, k3, p1, k13, p2.
Rnd 3: P2, C6B, k1, C6F, p1, RT, k1, p1, C6B, k1, C6F, p2.
Rnd 4: Rep Rnd 2.
Repeat Rnds 1-4 for left side panel in the rnd.

Worked flat
Row 1: (RS) P2, k13, p1, k1, LT, p1, k13, p2.
Row 2: K2, p13, k1, p3, k1, p13, k2.
Row 3: P2, C6B, k1, C6F, p1, RT, k1, p1, C6B, k1, C6F, p2.
Row 4: Rep Row 2.
Repeat Rows 1-4 for left side panel worked flat.

Center cable (multiple of 8 stitches)
See also chart, page 70.
Worked in the rnd
Rnds 1 and 2: Knit.
Rnd 3: *C4B, C4F; rep from *.
Rnds 4-6: Knit.
Rnd 7: *C4F, C4B; rep from *.
Rnd 8: Knit.
Repeat Rnds 1-8 for center cable in the rnd.

Worked flat
Row 1: (RS) Knit.
Row 2 and all WS rows: Purl.
Row 3: *C4B, C4F; rep from *.
Row 5: Knit.
Row 7: *C4F, C4B; rep from *.
Row 8: (WS) Purl.
Repeat Rows 1-8 for center cable worked flat.

Notes
Pullover is worked in the round from the bottom up. Front and back are separated at underarm. At underarm stitches are added at each edge to extend bodice. Then back and front are worked flat to the shoulders. Shoulders are shaped with short rows, then joined with WS together using an exposed three-needle bind off. Sleeves stitches are picked up around the armhole and knitted in the round to the cuff. Neck band is picked up around the neck edge and worked in garter stitch.

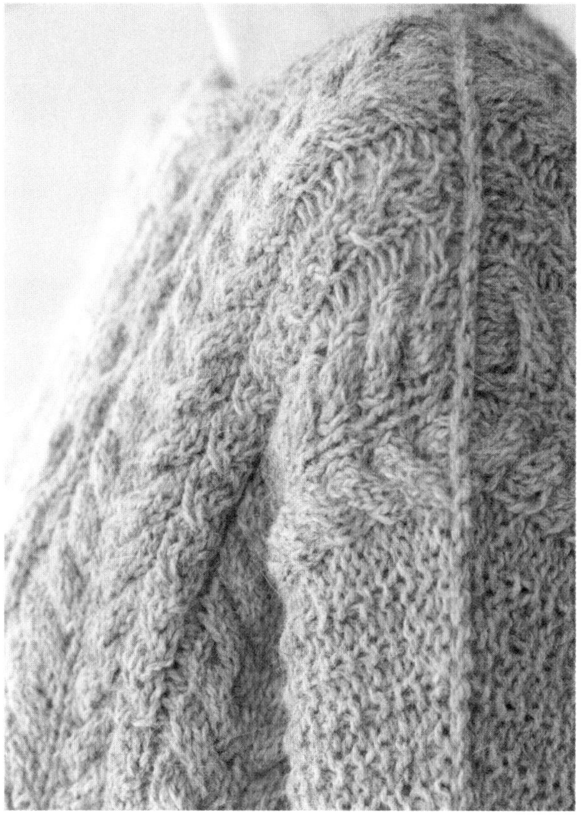

pullover

With smallest circular needle (circ) and using the long-tail cast on, CO 200 (212, 224, 236, 248, 260, 272, 288, 300, 312) sts. Place marker (pm) for beg of rnd (BOR) and join to work in the rnd, careful not to twist sts.

Begin ribbed border
First rnd: *K1, p1; rep from * to end.
Cont in est rib for 1¼" [3 cm].
Change to largest circ.
Next rnd *inc/dec rnd:* *(K1, p1) 4 (4, 2, 4, 3, 2, 1, 2, 1, 1) time(s), k1, k2tog, (p1, k1) 3 (3, 3, 4, 4, 4, 3, 4, 4, 2) times, M1L, [(p1, k1) 5 (4, 4, 3, 3, 3, 3, 3, 3, 3) times, M1L] 3 (4, 5, 6, 7, 8, 9, 9, 10, 11) times, (p1, k1) two times, M1L, [(p1, k1) 5 (4, 4, 3, 3, 3, 3, 3, 3, 3) times, M1L] 3 (4, 5, 6, 7, 8, 9, 9, 10, 11) times, (p1, k1) 3 (4, 3, 5, 4, 3, 3, 4, 3, 2) times, k2tog, (p1, k1) 4 (4, 2, 4, 3, 2, 1, 2, 1, 1) time(s), k2tog, p1; rep from * one more time to end; 6 sts dec'd and 16 (20, 24, 28, 32, 36, 40, 40, 44, 48) sts inc'd—210 (226, 242, 258, 274, 290, 306, 322, 338, 354) sts.

Begin cable patterns
Note: Place markers to help orient the first few rnds. After cable panels are established, you can remove setup markers, if you like, but leave side and BOR markers.
Next rnd *place markers:* *(P1, k1) 3 (5, 5, 7, 9, 11, 11, 13, 15, 17) times, pm for panel, work Rnd 1 of right side panel over 35 sts, pm for panel, work Rnd 1 of center cable over 24 (24, 32, 32, 32, 32, 40, 40, 40, 40) sts, pm for panel, work Rnd 1 of left side panel over 35 sts,

pm for panel, (k1, p1) 2 (4, 4, 6, 8, 10, 10, 12, 14, 16) times, k1, pm for side; rep from * one more time to end (BOR counts as second side marker).

Next rnd: *Purl to marker (m), slip marker (sl m), work Rnd 2 of right side panel to next m, sl m, work Rnd 2 of center cable to next m, sl m, work Rnd 2 of left side panel to next m, sl m, purl to side m, sl m; rep from * one more time.

Next rnd: *(P1, k1) to m, sl m, work next rnd of right side panel, sl m, work next rnd of center cable, sl m, work next rnd of left side panel, sl m, k1, (p1, k1) to side m; rep from * one more time.

Cont in est patts until pc meas approx 13½ (13½, 13½, 13½, 14, 14, 14, 14, 14½, 14½)" [34.5 (34.5, 34.5, 34.5, 35.5, 35.5, 35.5, 35.5, 37, 37) cm] from beg, ending after an even-numbered rnd of patts. Make note of last rnd worked in each patt.

Separate front and back

Next rnd *cast on rnd:* (RS) Place a locking st marker into the first st of the rnd, then using the cable cast on, CO 7 sts, k1, (p1, k1) to m, sl m, work patts as est to last panel m, sl m, k1, (p1, k1) to side m, place a locking st marker into the first st of second side, then place rem sts (including marked st) onto waste yarn for back.

Front

Next row *cast on row:* (WS) Using the cable cast on, CO 7 sts, pick up and knit 1 st in marked st from back, remove locking stitch marker, knit to m, sl m, work next WS row of each patt to last panel m, knit to end—120 (128, 136, 144, 152, 160, 168, 176, 184, 192) sts.

Next row: (RS) K1, (p1, k1) to m, sl m, work next RS row of each patt to last panel m, sl m, k1, (p1, k1) to end.

Next row: Knit to m, sl m, work next WS row of each patt to last panel m, sl m, knit to end.

Cont as est until pc meas approx 3½ (4, 4, 4½, 5, 5½, 6, 6½, 7, 7½)" [9 (10, 10, 11.5, 12.5, 14, 15, 16.5, 18, 19) cm] from underarm, ending after Row 3 of each side panel.

Place a locking st marker on either side of center 8 (8, 12, 12, 12, 12, 16, 16, 16, 16) sts for neck.

Begin front neck shaping

Note: Maintain pattern in center cable when possible. When not possible, work sts in stockinette. Do not count yarnovers as stitches.

Next row *bind off and dec row:* (WS) Work as est to neck m, remove m, join new ball of yarn and BO all sts to next m as follows (where it says to BO 1, pass the first stitch on the RH needle over the second stitch, do not work more stitches): P1, p2tog, BO 1, (p1, BO 1, p1, BO 1, p2tog, BO 1) 1 (1, 2, 2, 2, 2, 3, 3, 3, 3) times, p1, BO 1, remove m, p1, BO 1, work as est to end—56 (60, 62, 66, 70, 74, 76, 80, 84, 88) sts rem each side.

Next row *dec row:* (RS) Work in est patts to 2 sts before left neck edge, ssk; on right neck edge, k2tog, work in est patts to end (2 sts dec'd)—55 (59, 61, 65, 69, 73, 75, 79, 83, 87) sts each side.

Next row: (WS) Work to neck edge; then work to end.

Rep the last 2 rows two more times—53 (57, 59, 63, 67, 71, 73, 77, 81, 85) sts rem each side. Place a locking st marker at beg and end of last row worked.

Continue neck shaping and begin shoulder shaping

Next row *short row 1:* (RS) Work in est patts to 2 sts before neck edge, ssk; then k2tog, work in est patts to last 3 (4, 4, 6, 7, 9, 9, 10, 11, 13) sts, turn; (WS) yo, work to neck edge; then work to last 3 (4, 4, 6, 7, 9, 9, 10, 11, 13) sts, turn—52 (56, 58, 62, 66, 70, 72, 76, 80, 84) sts rem each side.

Next row *short row 2:* (RS) Yo, work to 2 sts before neck edge, ssk; then k2tog, work to 3 (4, 4, 6, 7, 8, 8, 10, 11, 12) sts before last gap, turn; (WS) yo, work to neck edge; then work to 3 (4, 4, 6, 7, 8, 8, 10, 11, 12) sts before last gap, turn—51 (55, 57, 61, 65, 69, 71, 75, 79, 83) sts rem each side.

Next row *short row 3:* (RS) Yo, work to 2 sts before neck edge, ssk; then k2tog, work to 3 (5, 5, 5, 7, 8, 8, 9, 11, 12) sts before last gap, turn; (WS) yo, work to neck edge; then work to 3 (5, 5, 5, 7, 8, 8, 9, 11, 12) sts before last gap, turn—50 (54, 56, 60, 64, 68, 70, 74, 78, 82) sts rem each side.

Next row *short row 4:* (RS) Yo, work to 2 sts before neck edge, ssk; then k2tog, work to 5 sts before last gap, turn; (WS) yo, k1, p1, p2tog, p3, work to neck edge; then work to 12 sts before last gap, p1, p2tog, p3, k1, turn—48, 52, 54, 58, 62, 66, 68, 72, 76, 80) sts rem each side.

Next row *short row 5:* (RS) Yo, work to neck edge; then work to 6 sts before last gap, turn; (WS) yo, k1, p1, p2tog, p3, work to neck edge; then work to 13 sts before last gap, p1, p2tog, p3, k1, turn—47 (51, 53, 57, 61, 65, 67, 71, 75, 79) sts rem each side.

Next row *short row 6:* (RS) Yo, work to neck edge; then work to 6 sts before last gap, turn; (WS) yo, work to neck edge; then work to 6 sts before last gap, turn.
Rep *short rows 4-6* one more time—44 (48, 50, 54, 58, 62, 64, 68, 72, 76) sts rem each side.

Resolve short rows
Next row: (RS) Yo, work to neck edge, turn; (WS) work in patts to end, working ssk or ssp to join each yo with st the after gap, keeping in patt.
Break yarn at left armhole edge. Place sts onto waste yarn.
Next row: (RS) With yarn attached at right shoulder, work in patts to end, working k2tog or p2tog in pattern to join each yo with the st after gap.
Break yarn. Place sts onto waste yarn.

Back
Return sts held for back to largest circ.
First row *pick up row:* (RS) With RS of back facing and beg at right armhole edge, pick up and knit 7 sts in underarm CO sts, (p1, k1) to m, sl m, work next RS row of each patt to last panel m, sl m, k1, (p1, k1) to end, then pick up and knit 1 st in marked st from front, remove locking stitch marker, then pick up and knit 7 sts in underarm CO—120 (128, 136, 144, 152, 160, 168, 176, 184, 192) sts on needle. Place a locking st marker at beg and end of this row.
Next row: (WS) Knit to m, sl m, work next WS row of each patt to last panel m, knit to end.
Next row: K1, (p1, k1) to m, sl m, work next RS row of each patt to last panel m, sl m, k1, (p1, k1) to end.
Cont in patts until pc meas same as front between markers at armhole edge, ending after Row 3 of each side panel.
Place a locking st marker on either side of center 24 (24, 28, 28, 28, 28, 32, 32, 32, 32) sts for neck.
Next row: (WS) Work in est patts to end.

Begin shoulder shaping
Next row *short row 1:* (RS) Work in est patts to last 3 (4, 4, 6, 7, 9, 9, 10, 11, 13) sts, turn; (WS) yo, work in est patts to last 3 (4, 4, 6, 7, 9, 9, 10, 11, 13) sts, turn.
Next row *short row 2:* (RS) Yo, work to 3 (4, 4, 6, 7, 8, 8, 10, 11, 12) sts before last gap, turn; (WS) yo, work to 3 (4, 4, 6, 7, 8, 8, 10, 11, 12) sts before last gap, turn.
Next row *short row 3:* (RS) Yo, work to 3 (5, 5, 5, 7, 8, 8, 9, 11, 12) sts before last gap, turn; (WS) yo, work to 3 (5, 5, 5, 7, 8, 8, 9, 11, 12) sts before last gap, turn.
Next row *short row 4:* (RS) Yo, work to 5 sts before last gap, turn; (WS) yo, k1, p1, p2tog, p3, work to 12 sts before last gap, p1, p2tog, p3, k1, turn—118 (126, 134, 142, 150, 158, 166, 174, 182, 190) sts rem.
Next row *short row 5:* (RS) Yo, work to neck edge; then work to 6 sts before last gap, turn; (WS) yo, k1, p1, p2tog, p3, work to 13 sts before last gap, p1, p2tog, p3, k1, turn—116 (124, 132, 140, 148, 156, 164, 172, 180, 188) sts rem.
Next row *short row 6:* (RS) Yo, work to 6 sts before last gap, turn; (WS) yo, work to 6 sts before last gap, turn.
Rep *short rows 4 and 5* one more time—112 (120, 128, 136, 144, 152, 160, 168, 176, 184) sts rem.
Next row *short row 7:* (RS) Yo, work to last 6 sts, turn; (WS) yo, work to neck m, remove m and BO all sts to next m as follows: P1, p2tog, BO 1, (p1, BO 1, p1, BO 1, p2tog, BO 1) 5 (5, 6, 6, 6, 6, 7, 7, 7, 7) times, p1, BO 1, remove m, p1, BO 1, then work to 6 sts before last gap, turn—44 (48, 50, 54, 58, 62, 64, 68, 72, 76) sts rem each side.

Resolve short rows
Next row: (RS) Yo, work to neck edge, turn.
Next row: (WS) Work to end, working ssk or ssp in pattern to join each yo with the st after gap.
Break yarn leaving a tail roughly five times the width of the shoulder for finishing. Join yarn at left neck edge, ready to work a RS row.
Next row: (RS) Work to end, working k2tog or p2tog in pattern to join each yo with the st after gap. Do not break yarn.

Join shoulders
Place sts held for front shoulders onto smaller circ. With WS of pcs held tog and yarn attached at left armhole edge, using the three-needle bind off, BO all left shoulder sts. With long tail at right armhole edge, rep for right shoulder.

Gently steam block piece.

Sleeves

With RS facing and larger double-pointed needles (dpns), beg at underarm, pick up and knit 18 (20, 20, 22, 24, 26, 28, 30, 32, 34) sts along armhole edge to shoulder seam (approx 2 sts for every 3 rows) then pick up and knit 18 (20, 20, 22, 24, 26, 28, 30, 32, 34) sts to underarm—36 (40, 40, 44, 48, 52, 56, 60, 64, 68) sts on needles. Pm for BOR.

Begin garter rib

Rnd 1: K1, *p2, k2; rep from * to last 3 sts, p2, k1.
Rnd 2: Knit.
Rep the last 2 rnds four more times, then work Rnd 1 one more time.

Begin sleeve shaping

Next rnd *dec rnd:* K1, k2tog, knit to last 3 sts, ssk, k1 (2 sts dec'd)—34 (38, 38, 42, 46, 50, 54, 58, 62, 66) sts.
Cont in est patt and work *dec rnd* every 20 (10, 10, 8, 8, 6, 4, 4, 4, 4) rnds 2 (4, 4, 6, 6, 8, 10, 10, 12, 14) more times—30 (30, 30, 30, 34, 34, 34, 38, 38, 38) sts.
Cont in est patt until sleeve meas 13½" [34.5 cm] from pick-up.
Next rnd: Bind off in pattern.

Finishing

Weave in ends. Gently steam block, plumping cables with your fingers to provide maximum texture.

Neck band

With RS facing and middle circ, beg at right shoulder seam, pick up and knit 1 st in each BO st and 1 st for every 2 rows around neck edge. Pm for BOR.

First rnd: Purl.
Next rnd: Knit.
Rep the last 2 rnds two more times.
Next rnd: Bind off purlwise.

Weave in rem ends, gently steam neck band.

Key

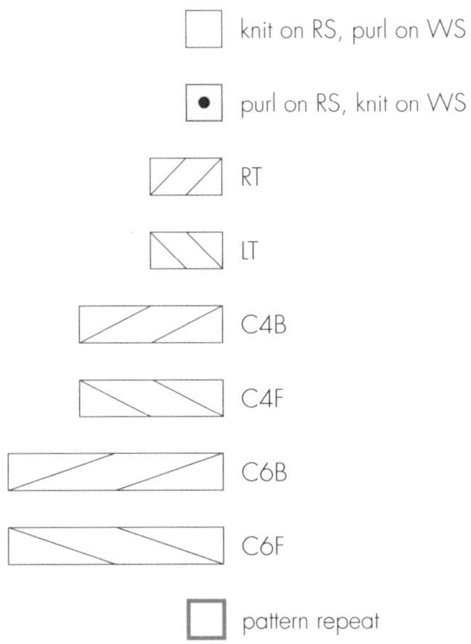

Texture pattern

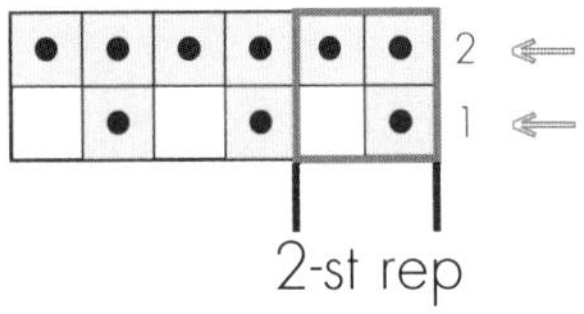

Center cable panel

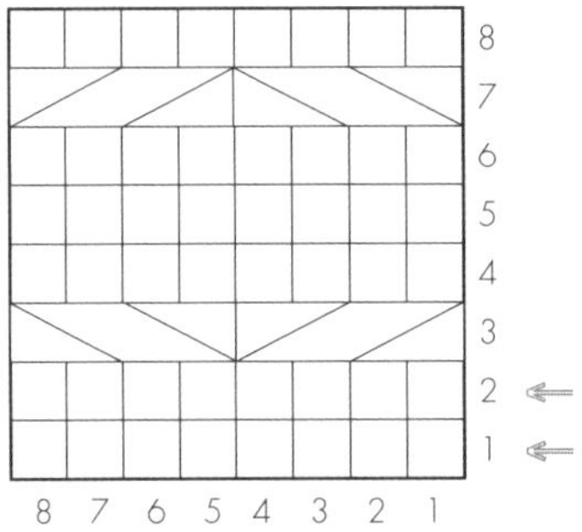

Right side panel

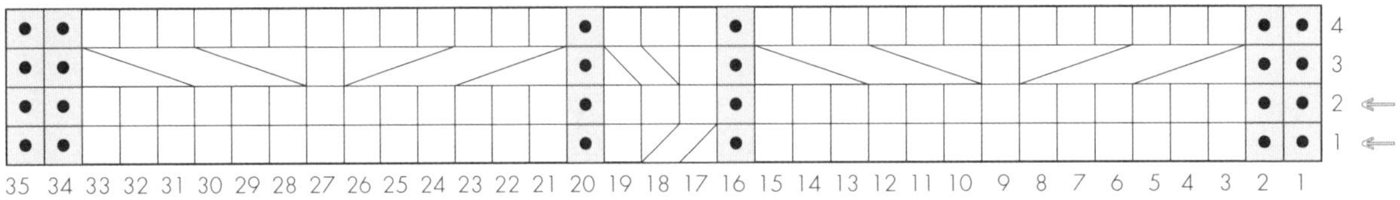

Note: When working flat, read even-numbered rows from left to right.

Left side panel

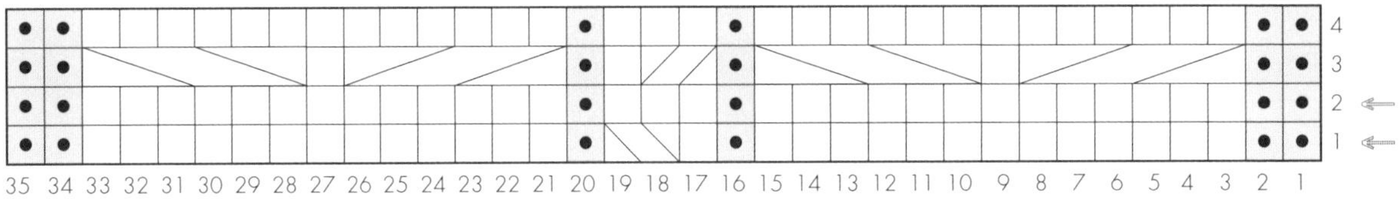

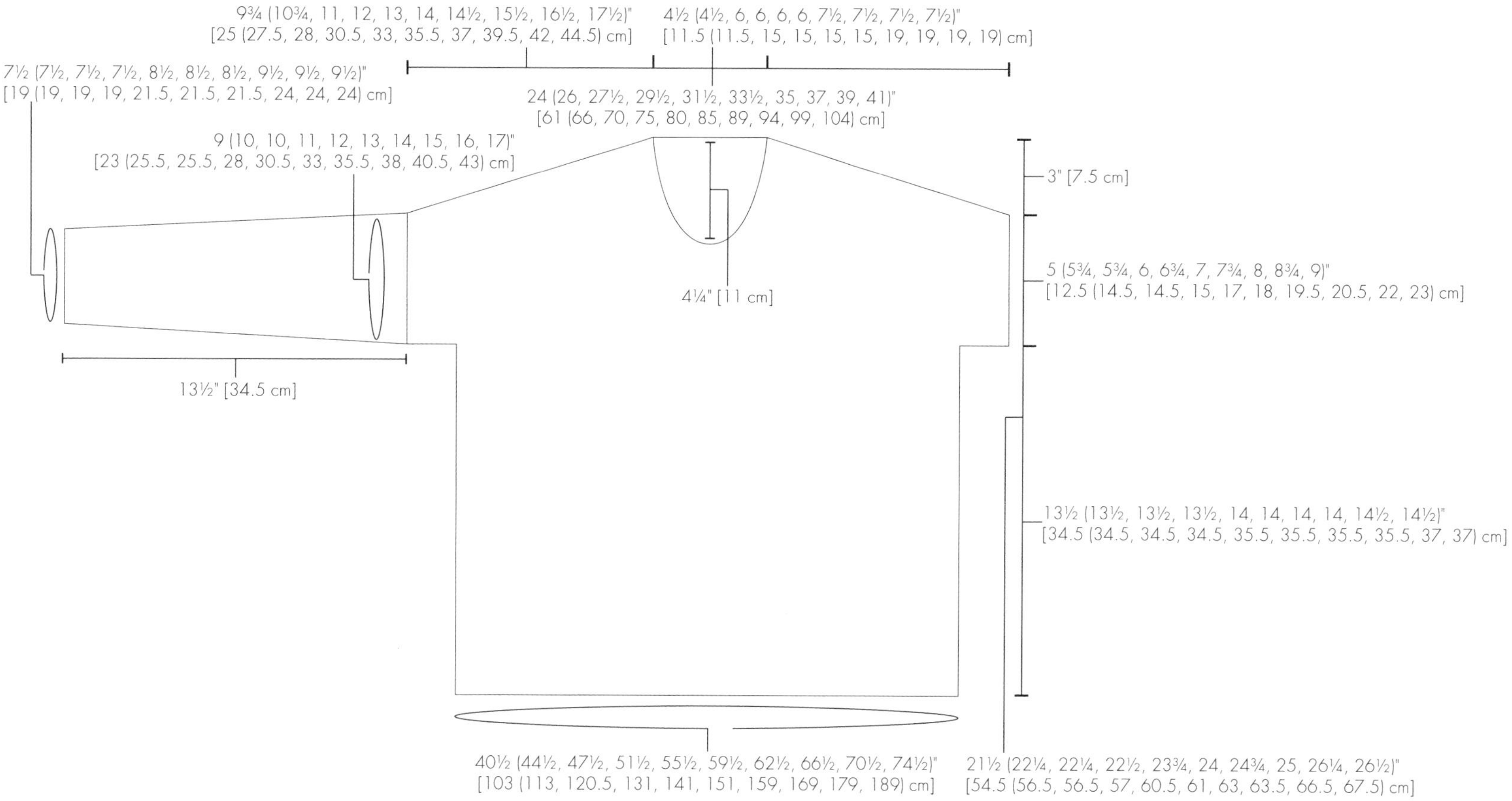
9¾ (10¾, 11, 12, 13, 14, 14½, 15½, 16½, 17½)"
[25 (27.5, 28, 30.5, 33, 35.5, 37, 39.5, 42, 44.5) cm]
4½ (4½, 6, 6, 6, 6, 7½, 7½, 7½, 7½)"
[11.5 (11.5, 15, 15, 15, 15, 19, 19, 19, 19) cm]
7½ (7½, 7½, 7½, 8½, 8½, 8½, 9½, 9½, 9½)"
[19 (19, 19, 19, 21.5, 21.5, 21.5, 24, 24, 24) cm]
24 (26, 27½, 29½, 31½, 33½, 35, 37, 39, 41)"
[61 (66, 70, 75, 80, 85, 89, 94, 99, 104) cm]
9 (10, 10, 11, 12, 13, 14, 15, 16, 17)"
[23 (25.5, 25.5, 28, 30.5, 33, 35.5, 38, 40.5, 43) cm]
3" [7.5 cm]
5 (5¾, 5¾, 6, 6¾, 7, 7¾, 8, 8¾, 9)"
[12.5 (14.5, 14.5, 15, 17, 18, 19.5, 20.5, 22, 23) cm]
4¼" [11 cm]
13½" [34.5 cm]
13½ (13½, 13½, 13½, 14, 14, 14, 14, 14½, 14½)"
[34.5 (34.5, 34.5, 34.5, 35.5, 35.5, 35.5, 35.5, 37, 37) cm]
40½ (44½, 47½, 51½, 55½, 59½, 62½, 66½, 70½, 74½)"
[103 (113, 120.5, 131, 141, 151, 159, 169, 179, 189) cm]
21½ (22¼, 22¼, 22½, 23¾, 24, 24¾, 25, 26¼, 26½)"
[54.5 (56.5, 56.5, 57, 60.5, 61, 63, 63.5, 66.5, 67.5) cm]

honeysuckle

I've always loved the traditional roomy peasant smock from Northern Europe, with wide sleeves gathered at the cuffs, and often seen with tucks and embroidery on the yoke's front. These smocks were sewn with woven fabric, of course, and sewn garments don't always translate well to knitwear. Sewing and knitting are different media, after all. But, in this instance, working Owlet, a fine yarn, on larger needles creates a fabric floaty and giving enough to drape well when gathered. Deeply tucked stitches on the yoke panel make a texture not unlike rustic embroidery.

Finished measurements
32½ (36¾, 40¾, 45, 49¼, 54¼, 58½, 62¾, 67¾, 72, 76¼)" [82.5 (93.5, 103.5, 114.5, 125, 138, 148.5, 159.5, 172, 183, 193.5) cm] bust circumference; shown in size 40¾" [103.5 cm] on a 31" [79 cm], 5'11" [180 cm] model (9¾" [25 cm] positive ease)

Yarn
Owlet by Quince & Co
(50% American wool, 50% alpaca; 240yd [220m]/50g)

- 5 (6, 6, 6, 7, 8, 8, 9, 10, 11, 12) skeins Tawny 302

Needles

- One 16" circular needle (circ) in size US 5 [3.75 mm]
- One 32" circ in size US 5 [3.75 mm]
- One 16" circ in size US 8 [5 mm]
- One 32" circ in size US 8 [5 mm]
- One set double-pointed needles (dpns) in size US 5 [3.75 mm]
- One set dpns in size US 8 [5 mm]

Or size to obtain gauge

Notions

- Stitch markers
- Locking stitch markers
- Waste yarn
- Tapestry needle

Gauge
19 sts and 30 rnds = 4" [10 cm] in stockinette stitch on larger needle, after light steam blocking.

Panel set up
See also set up chart, page 76.
Rnd 1: P2, *sl1yo, p1, sl1yo, p5; rep from * to 5 sts before panel marker (m), sl1yo, p1, sl1yo, p2.
Rnd 2: P2, *brk, p1, brk, p5; rep from * to 5 sts before m, brk, p1, brk, p2.
Rnd 3: Rep Rnd 1.
Rnd 4: P2, *brk, p1, brk, p2, sl1yo, p2; rep from * to 5 sts before m, brk, p1, brk, p2.
Rnd 5: P2, *sl1yo, p1, sl1yo, p2, sl1yo slipping the st and yo from previous row, p2; rep from * to 5 sts before m, sl1yo, p1, sl1yo, p2.

Yoke panel (multiple of 8 sts + 7)
See also panel chart, page 76.
Set up row: (WS) K2, sl1yo, k1, sl1yo, *k5, sl1yo, k1, sl1yo; rep from * to 2 sts before m, k2.
Row 1: (RS) P2, *brk, p1, brk, p2, sl1yo, p2; rep from * to 5 sts before m, brk, p1, brk, p2.
Row 2: (WS) K2, sl1yo, k1, sl1yo, *k2, sl1yo slipping the st and yo from previous row, k2, sl1yo, k1, sl1yo; rep from * to 2 sts before m, k2.
Row 3: P2, *brk, p1, brk, p2, sl1yo slipping the st and yos from previous two rows, p2; rep from * to 5 sts before m, brk, p1, brk, p2.
Row 4: K2, sl1yo, k1, sl1yo, *k2, sl1yo slipping the st and yos from previous three rows, k2, sl1yo, k1, sl1yo; rep from * to 2 sts before m, k2.
Row 5: P2, *brk, p1, brk, p2, sl1yo slipping the st and yos from previous four rows, p2; rep from * to 5 sts before m, brk, p1, brk, p2.
Row 6: K2, sl1yo, k1, sl1yo, *k2, sl1yo slipping the st and yos from previous five rows, k2, sl1yo, k1, sl1yo; rep from * to 2 sts before m, k2.

Row 7: P2, *brk, p1, brk, p2, brk slipping the st and yos from previous six rows, p2; rep from * to 5 sts before m, brk, p1, brk, p2.
Row 8: K2, sl1yo, k1, sl1yo, *k2, p1, k2, sl1yo, k1, sl1yo; rep from * to 2 sts before m, k2.
Row 9: P2, *brk, p1, brk, p5; rep from * to 5 sts before m, brk, p1, brk, p2.
Row 10: K2, sl1yo, k1, sl1yo, *k5, sl1yo, k1, sl1yo; rep from * to 2 sts before m, k2.
Rows 11 and 12: Rep Rows 9 and 10.
Rep Rows 1-12 for yoke panel.

Notes

1. Pullover is knitted in the round from the bottom up. Front and back are separated at the underarm. At underarm, stitches are added at each side edge to extend bodice, then pieces are worked flat to the shoulders. Shoulders are shaped with short rows, then joined with WS together using an exposed three-needle bind off. Sleeves stitches are picked up around the armhole and knitted in the round to the cuff. For the neck band, stitches are picked up around the neck edge and worked in rib pattern.
2. Yoke stitch pattern begins in the round. After front and back are separated, the pattern is worked back and forth. When working the stitch pattern, all slipped stitches are slipped with the yarn to the WS of work.

pullover

With smaller, longer circular needle (circ) and using the long-tail cast on, CO 206 (230, 254, 278, 302, 338, 362, 386, 422, 446, 470) sts. Place marker (pm) for beg of rnd (BOR) and join to work in the rnd, careful not to twist sts.

Begin ribbed border

First rnd: *K1, p1; rep from * to end.
Cont in est rib patt for 3 more rnds.
Next rnd *dec rnd:* *K1, p1, k1, k2tog, p1; rep from * to last 2 sts, k1, p1; 34 (38, 42, 46, 50, 56, 60, 64, 70, 74, 78) sts dec'd—172 (192, 212, 232, 252, 282, 302, 322, 352, 372, 392) sts rem.
Change to larger circ.

Begin stockinette stitch

Next rnd *place markers:* K95 (105, 115, 125, 135, 153, 163, 173, 191, 201, 211), pm for side, k77 (87, 97, 107, 117, 129, 139, 149, 161, 171, 181) back sts to end (BOR counts as second side marker, front begins with more sts than back).
Cont in St st until pc meas 11½ (11½, 11½, 12, 12, 12, 12½, 12½, 12½, 13, 13)" [29 (29, 29, 30.5, 30.5, 30.5, 32, 32, 32, 33, 33) cm] from beg.
Next rnd *place markers:* K19 (20, 25, 30, 35, 37, 42, 47, 49, 54, 59), pm for panel, k57 (65, 65, 65, 65, 79, 79, 79, 93, 93, 93), pm for panel, k19 (20, 25, 30, 35, 37, 42, 47, 49, 54, 59) to side m, sl m, knit to end.

Begin yoke panel set up

Next rnd *dec rnd:* Knit to panel m, sl m, k5 (9, 9, 9, 9, 8, 8, 8, 7, 7, 7), *k2tog, k1, (k2tog) two times, k1; rep from * to 4 (8, 8, 8, 8, 7, 7, 7, 6, 6, 6) sts before panel m, knit to end; 18 (18, 18, 18, 18, 24, 24, 24, 30, 30, 30) sts dec'd—154 (174, 194, 214, 234, 258, 278, 298, 322, 342, 362) sts rem: 77 (87, 97, 107, 117, 129, 139, 149, 161, 171, 181) sts each for front and back, and 39 (47, 47, 47, 47, 55, 55, 55, 63, 63, 63) sts in panel.
Next rnd *bind off and pick up rnd:* Knit to panel m, with a new ball of yarn, BO all sts to next panel m, removing marker to BO last st, then place last st made onto LH needle, break yarn, with RH needle and main yarn, pick up and knit 1 st in each of next 39 (47, 47, 47, 47, 55, 55, 55, 63, 63, 63) BO sts, pm for panel, slip next st purlwise, then knit to end—154 (174, 194, 214, 234, 258, 278, 298, 322, 342, 362) sts; 77 (87, 97, 107, 117, 129, 139, 149, 161, 171, 181) sts each for front and back; 39 (47, 47, 47, 47, 55, 55, 55, 63, 63, 63) sts in panel.

Begin yoke panel patterns

Next rnd: Knit to panel m, sl m, work Rnd 1 of panel set up to next m, sl m, knit to end.

Begin underarm shaping and continue panel patterns

Next rnd *inc rnd:* K1, M1R, knit to panel m, sl m, work next rnd of panel set up, sl m, knit to 1 st before side m, M1L, k1, sl m, k1, M1R, knit to last st, M1L, k1 (4 sts inc'd)—158 (178, 198, 218, 238, 262, 282, 302, 326, 346, 366) sts.
Cont in St st and panel set up through Rnd 5.

Separate front and back

Next row: (RS) Using the cable cast on, CO 7 sts, knit to panel m, sl m, work Row 3 of yoke panel to next m, sl m, knit to side m, then place rem sts for back onto waste yarn.

Place a locking st marker at beg and end of row just worked.

Front

Next row: (WS) Using the cable cast on, CO 7 sts, purl to panel m, sl m, work Row 4 of yoke panel to next m, sl m, purl to end—93 (103, 113, 123, 133, 145, 155, 165, 177, 187, 197) sts.

Cont as est in St st and yoke panel through Row 12, work Rows 1-12 of panel 3 (4, 4, 4, 5, 5, 5, 6, 6, 7, 7) more times, then work Rows 1-8 one more time. Place a locking st marker at beg and end of last row worked, then work Row 9 of panel.

Next row: (WS) Purl to panel m, sl m, work 13 (17, 18, 17, 17, 22, 22, 22, 25, 26, 26) sts in patt, pm for neck, work 13 (13, 11, 13, 13, 11, 11, 11, 13, 11, 11) sts in patt, pm for neck, work 13 (17, 18, 17, 17, 22, 22, 22, 25, 26, 26) sts in patt, sl m, purl to end.

Pc meas approx 7½ (9, 9, 9, 10¾, 10¾, 10¾, 12¼, 12¼, 13¾, 13¾)" [19 (23, 23, 23, 27.5, 27.5, 27.5, 31, 31, 35, 35) cm] from underarm.

Begin neck and shoulder shaping

Note: Do not count yarnovers as stitches. Maintain pattern as best you can through neck shaping. If short rows end between panel Rows 1 and 7 for your size, work final RS short row as Row 7 to resolve all slipped stitches.

Next row *short row 1:* (RS) Knit to panel m, work next row of panel to neck m, remove m, join a new ball of yarn and BO all sts to next m, removing marker to BO last st, work panel to next m, sl m, knit to last 4 (4, 5, 5, 5, 5, 6, 6, 6, 6, 6) sts, turn—40 (45, 51, 55, 60, 67, 72, 77, 82, 88, 93) sts rem for each side; (WS) yo, work as est to right neck edge; on left neck edge, BO 3 sts, work as est to last 4 (4, 5, 5, 5, 5, 6, 6, 6, 6, 6) sts, turn.

Next row *short row 2:* (RS) Yo, work in est patts to neck edge; then BO 3 sts, work in est patts to 4 (4, 4, 5, 5, 5, 5, 5, 6, 6, 6) sts before last gap, turn—37 (42, 48, 52, 57, 64, 69, 74, 79, 85, 90) sts each side; (WS) yo, work in est patts to neck edge; then BO 3 (3, 2, 3, 3, 2, 2, 2, 2, 3, 2) sts, work in est patts to 4 (4, 4, 5, 5, 5, 5, 5, 6, 6, 6) sts before last gap, turn.

Next row *short row 3:* (RS) Yo, work to neck edge; then BO 3 (3, 2, 3, 3, 2, 2, 2, 2, 3, 2) sts, work to 4 (4, 4, 4, 5, 5, 5, 5, 5, 5, 5) sts before last gap, turn; (WS) yo, work to neck edge; on left neck edge work as est to 4 (4, 4, 4, 5, 5, 5, 5, 5, 5, 5) sts before last gap, turn—34 (39, 46, 49, 54, 62, 67, 72, 77, 82, 88) sts rem each side.

Next row *short row 4:* (RS) Yo, work to 2 sts before neck edge, ssk; then k2tog, work to 4 (4, 4, 4, 5, 5, 5, 5, 5, 5, 5) sts before last gap, turn; (WS) yo, work to neck edge; then work to 4 (4, 4, 4, 5, 5, 5, 5, 5, 5, 5) sts before last gap, turn—33 (38, 45, 48, 53, 61, 66, 71, 76, 81, 87) sts rem each side.

Rep *short row four* 1 (1, 2, 3, 3, 3, 4, 5, 5, 6, 7) more time(s)—32 (37, 43, 45, 50, 58, 62, 66, 71, 75, 80) sts rem each side.

Next row *short row 5:* (RS) Yo, work to neck edge; then work to 4 (4, 4, 4, 4, 5, 5, 5, 5, 5, 5) sts before last gap, turn; (WS) yo, work to neck edge; then work to 4 (4, 4, 4, 4, 5, 5, 5, 5, 5, 5) sts before gap, turn.

Next row *short row 6:* (RS) Yo, work to 2 sts before neck edge, ssk; then k2tog, work to 3 (4, 4, 4, 4, 5, 4, 4, 5, 5, 5) sts before last gap, turn; (WS) yo, work to neck edge; then work to 3 (4, 4, 4, 4, 5, 4, 4, 5, 5, 5) sts before last gap, turn—31 (36, 42, 44, 49, 57, 61, 65, 70, 74, 79) sts rem each side.

Resolve short rows

Next row: (RS) Yo, work to neck edge, turn; (WS) purl to end, working ssp to join each yo with the st after gap.

Break yarn at left shoulder. Place sts onto waste yarn.

Next row: (RS) With yarn attached at right shoulder, knit to end, working k2tog to join each yo with the st after gap.

Break yarn. Place sts onto waste yarn.

Back

Return sts held for back to larger circ.

Next row: (RS) With RS of back facing and beg at right armhole edge, pick up and knit 7 sts in underarm CO from right front, knit across back sts, then pick up and knit 7 sts in underarm CO from left front—93 (103, 113, 123, 133, 145, 155, 165, 177, 187, 197) sts.

Next row: (WS) Purl.

Cont in St st until back meas same as front between locking st markers, ending after a WS row.

Next row *place markers:* (RS) K27 (28, 33, 38, 43, 45, 50, 55, 57, 62, 67), pm for panel, k4 (8, 9, 6, 6, 12, 11, 10, 13, 12, 12), pm for neck, k31 (31, 29, 35, 35, 31, 33, 35, 37, 39, 39), pm for neck, k4 (8, 9, 6, 6, 12, 11, 10, 13, 12, 12), pm for panel, k27 (28, 33, 38, 43, 45, 50, 55, 57, 62, 67) sts to end.

Begin yoke pattern

Next row: (WS) Purl to panel m, sl m, work set up row for yoke panel to next panel m (slipping neck markers), sl m, purl to end.

Begin shoulder shaping

Note: Do not count yarnovers as stitches. If short rows end between panel Rows 1 and 7 for your size, work final RS short row as Row 7 to resolve all slipped stitches.

Next row *short row 1:* (RS) Knit to panel m, sl m, work Row 1 of yoke panel to next panel m, sl m, knit to last 4 (4, 5, 5, 5, 5, 6, 6, 6, 6, 6) sts, turn; (WS) yo, purl to panel m, sl m, work Row 2 of panel to next panel m, sl m, purl to last 4 (4, 5, 5, 5, 6, 6, 6, 6, 6) sts, turn.

Next row *short row 2:* (RS) Yo, work in est patts to 4 (4, 4, 5, 5, 5, 5, 5, 6, 6, 6) sts before last gap, turn; (WS) yo, work in est patts to 4 (4, 4, 5, 5, 5, 5, 5, 6, 6, 6) sts before last gap, turn.

Rep *short row two* 4 (5, 6, 0, 5, 7, 7, 8, 0, 0, 0) more times.

Sizes - (36¾, 40¾, -, -, 54¼, -, -, -, -, -)" [- (93.5, 103.5, -, -, 138, -, -, -, -, -) cm] only:

Proceed to All sizes.

Sizes 32½ (-, -, 45, 49¼, -, 58½, 62¾, 67¾, 72, 76¼)" [82.5 (-, -, 114.5, 125, -, 148.5, 159.5, 172, 183, 193.5) cm] only:

Next row *short row 3:* (RS) Yo, work to 3 (-, -, 4, 4, -, 4, 4, 5, 5, 5) sts before last gap, turn; (WS) yo, work to 3 (-, -, 4, 4, -, 4, 4, 5, 5, 5) sts before last gap, turn.

Rep *short row three* 0 (-, -, 6, 1, -, 0, 0, 8, 9, 10) more time(s).

All sizes

Resolve short rows

Next row: (RS) Yo, work as est to neck m, BO all sts to next neck m, removing marker to BO last st, then work as est to end, working k2tog to join each yo with the st after gap. Break yarn leaving a tail roughly five times the width of the shoulder for finishing. Join yarn at right neck edge, ready to work a WS row.

Next row: (WS) Work as est to end, working ssp to join each yo with the st after gap. Do not break yarn.

Join shoulders

Place sts held for left and right front shoulders onto smaller circ. With WS of pcs held tog and attached yarn, using the three-needle bind off, BO all left shoulder sts. With long tail at right armhole edge, rep for right shoulder.

Remove locking st markers that were used for measuring.

Gently steam block piece.

Sleeves

With RS facing and shorter, larger circ, beg at underarm, pick up and knit 40 (48, 48, 48, 56, 56, 56, 64, 64, 72, 72) sts to shoulder seam (approx 2 sts for every 3 rows), then pick up and knit 40 (48, 48, 48, 56, 56, 56, 64, 64, 72, 72) sts to underarm—80 (96, 96, 96, 112, 112, 112, 128, 128, 144, 144) sts on needle. Pm for BOR.

First rnd: Knit.

Cont in St st until pc meas 13½ (13½, 13½, 13, 13, 13, 12½, 12½, 12½, 12, 12)" [34.5 (34.5, 34.5, 33, 33, 33, 32, 32, 32, 30.5, 30.5) cm] from pick-up.

Begin cuff shaping

Note: Change to larger double-pointed needles (dpns) when necessary.

Next rnd *dec rnd:* *K8 (4, 4, 4, 2, 2, 2, 2, 2, 2, 2), k2tog; rep from * to end; 8 (16, 16, 16, 28, 28, 28, 32, 32, 36, 36) sts dec'd—72 (80, 80, 80, 84, 84, 84, 96, 96, 108, 108) sts rem.

Next rnd *dec rnd:* *K2tog; rep from * to end—36 (40, 40, 40, 42, 42, 42, 48, 48, 54, 54) sts rem.

Change to smaller dpns.

Begin ribbed cuff

First rnd: *K1, p1; rep from * to end.

Cont in est rib for 5 more rnds.

Next rnd: Bind off in pattern.

Finishing

Weave in ends. Very gently steam block, being careful not to flatten yoke panel pattern.

Neck band

With RS facing and smaller, shorter circ, beginning at right shoulder seam, pick up and knit 1 st in each BO st and 1 st in each row around neck edge, making sure to pick up an even number of sts. Pm for BOR.

First rnd: *K1, p1; rep from * to end.

Cont in rib for ¾" [2 cm].

Next rnd: Bind off in pattern.

Weave in rem ends and gently block again, if you like.

Key

- knit on RS, purl on WS
- purl on RS, knit on WS
- sl1yo on RS and WS
- brk
- pattern repeat

Panel set up

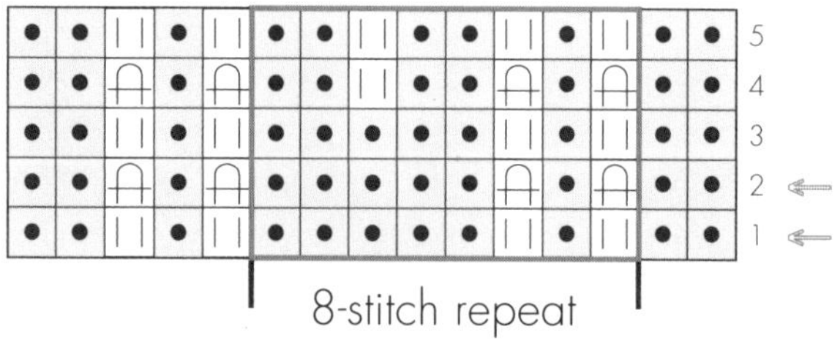

Yoke panel

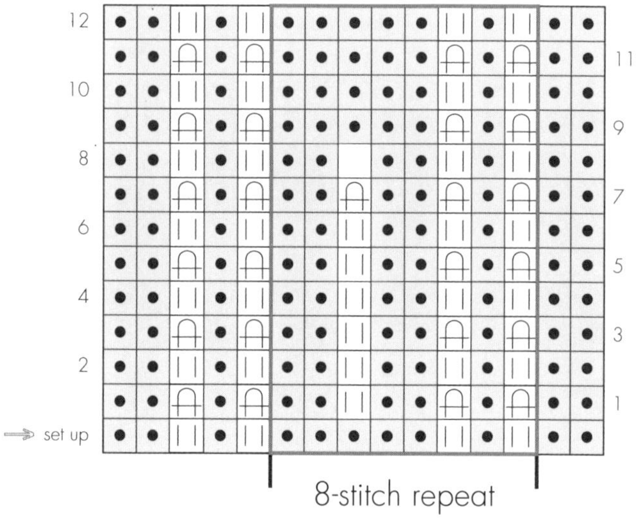

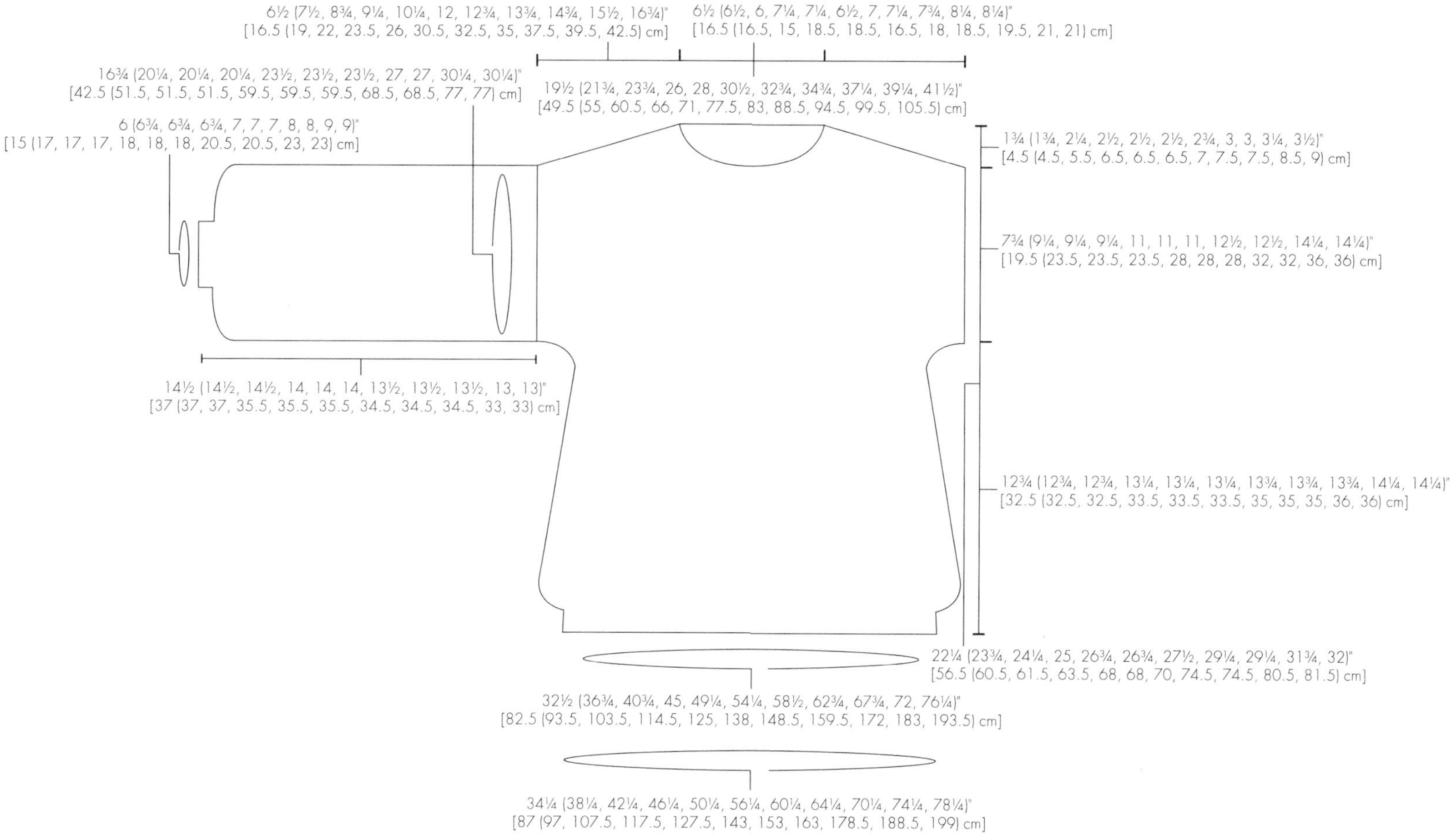
6½ (7½, 8¾, 9¼, 10¼, 12, 12¾, 13¾, 14¾, 15½, 16¾)"
[16.5 (19, 22, 23.5, 26, 30.5, 32.5, 35, 37.5, 39.5, 42.5) cm]
6½ (6½, 6, 7¼, 7¼, 6½, 7, 7¼, 7¾, 8¼, 8¼)"
[16.5 (16.5, 15, 18.5, 18.5, 16.5, 18, 18.5, 19.5, 21, 21) cm]
16¾ (20¼, 20¼, 20¼, 23½, 23½, 23½, 27, 27, 30¼, 30¼)"
[42.5 (51.5, 51.5, 51.5, 59.5, 59.5, 59.5, 68.5, 68.5, 77, 77) cm]
19½ (21¾, 23¾, 26, 28, 30½, 32¾, 34¾, 37¼, 39¼, 41½)"
[49.5 (55, 60.5, 66, 71, 77.5, 83, 88.5, 94.5, 99.5, 105.5) cm]
6 (6¾, 6¾, 6¾, 7, 7, 7, 8, 8, 9, 9)"
[15 (17, 17, 17, 18, 18, 18, 20.5, 20.5, 23, 23) cm]
1¾ (1¾, 2¼, 2½, 2½, 2½, 2¾, 3, 3, 3¼, 3½)"
[4.5 (4.5, 5.5, 6.5, 6.5, 6.5, 7, 7.5, 7.5, 8.5, 9) cm]
7¾ (9¼, 9¼, 9¼, 11, 11, 11, 12½, 12½, 14¼, 14¼)"
[19.5 (23.5, 23.5, 23.5, 28, 28, 28, 32, 32, 36, 36) cm]
14½ (14½, 14½, 14, 14, 14, 13½, 13½, 13½, 13, 13)"
[37 (37, 37, 35.5, 35.5, 35.5, 34.5, 34.5, 34.5, 33, 33) cm]
12¾ (12¾, 12¾, 13¼, 13¼, 13¼, 13¾, 13¾, 13¾, 14¼, 14¼)"
[32.5 (32.5, 32.5, 33.5, 33.5, 33.5, 35, 35, 35, 36, 36) cm]
22¼ (23¾, 24¼, 25, 26¾, 26¾, 27½, 29¼, 29¼, 31¾, 32)"
[56.5 (60.5, 61.5, 63.5, 68, 68, 70, 74.5, 74.5, 80.5, 81.5) cm]
32½ (36¾, 40¾, 45, 49¼, 54¼, 58½, 62¾, 67¾, 72, 76¼)"
[82.5 (93.5, 103.5, 114.5, 125, 138, 148.5, 159.5, 172, 183, 193.5) cm]
34¼ (38¼, 42¼, 46¼, 50¼, 56¼, 60¼, 64¼, 70¼, 74¼, 78¼)"
[87 (97, 107.5, 117.5, 127.5, 143, 153, 163, 178.5, 188.5, 199) cm]

sumac

The center front panel on this sweater is once again the result of swatching from Barbara Walker's stitch dictionaries. The pattern is called Austrian Block and uses a combination of twist and regular knit stitches for its blocks. Because the pattern is so vertical (and blocky) I've curved the outer edges at the neckline for a little softening of the overall effect.

Finished measurements
35¾ (40¼, 44¾, 49, 53½, 58, 62¼, 66¾, 71¼, 75½)" [91 (102, 113.5, 124.5, 136, 147.5, 158, 169.5, 181, 192) cm] bust circumference; shown in size 44¾" [113.5 cm] on a 31" [79 cm], 5'11" [180 cm] tall model (13¾" [35 cm] positive ease)

Yarn
Owl by Quince & Co
(50% American wool, 50% alpaca; 120yd [110m]/50g)

- 7 (8, 9, 9, 10, 11, 11, 12, 13, 13) skeins Abyssinian 309

Needles

- One 16" circular needle (circ) in size US 9 [5.5 mm]
- One 32" circ in size US 10 [6 mm]
- One set double-pointed needles in size US 10 [6 mm]

Or size to obtain gauge

Notions

- Cable needle (optional)
- Stitch markers
- Waste yarn
- Tapestry needle

Gauge
14½ sts and 24 rnds = 4" [10 cm] in stockinette stitch with larger needle, after gentle steam blocking
Center panel (35 sts) = 8" [20.5 cm] wide.

Panel setup (35 stitches)
See also chart, page 83.
Rnd 1: P2, k1, *p4, k1; rep from * to 2 sts before marker (m), p2.
Rnds 2 and 3: Rep Rnd 1.
Rnd 4: P2, k1, *p2, k5, p2, k1; rep from * to 2 sts before m, p2.

Austrian Block panel (35 stitches)
See also chart, page 83.
Worked in the rnd
Rnd 1: P2, k1, *p2, RT, k1, LT, p2, k1; rep from * to 2 sts before m, p2.
Rnd 2: P2, k1, *p2, k5, p2, k1; rep from * to 2 sts before m, p2.
Rnds 3-8: Rep Rnds 1 and 2 three times.
Rnd 9: Rep Rnd 1.
Rnd 10: P2, k1, *k2, p2, k1, p2, k3; rep from * to 2 sts before m, p2.
Rnd 11: P2, k1, *LT, p2, k1, p2, RT, k1; rep from * to 2 sts before m, p2.
Rnds 12-19: Rep Rnds 10 and 11 four times.
Rnd 20: Rep Rnd 2.
Repeat Rnds 1-20 for Austrian Block panel.

Worked flat
Row 1: (RS) P2, k1, *p2, RT, k1, LT, p2, k1; rep from * to 2 sts before m, p2.
Row 2: K2, *p1, k2, p5, k2; rep from * to 3 sts before m, p1, k2.
Rows 3-8: Rep Rows 1 and 2 three times.
Row 9: (RS) Rep Row 1.
Row 10: K2, *p3, k2, p1, k2, p2; rep from * to 3 sts before m, p1, k2.

> Row gauge is important in this sweater. The center panel pattern stitch is intimately connected to the shaping. After the front neckline bind off, the neckline shaping decreases are worked at either side of the pattern panel, not directly on the neck edge. To make things easy, we've charted the back panel shaping for you. The down side of being this specific is that if your row gauge is significantly different from that stated in the pattern, your length measurements may vary from those in the schematic.

Row 11: P2, k1, *LT, p2, k1, p2, RT, k1; rep from * to 2 sts before m, p2.
Rows 12-19: Rep Rows 10 and 11 four times.
Row 20: Rep Row 2.
Repeat Rows 1-20 for Austrian Block panel.

Increase panel (35 sts, inc'd to 47 sts)

Note: Not all sizes will work all of the rows of the increase panel. Work panel to resolution of short row shaping on back.
See also chart, page 83.
Row 1 *inc row:* (RS) P2, k1, LT, p2, k1, p2, RT, k1, LT, p2, m1-p/L, k1, m1-p/L, p2, RT, k1, LT, p2, k1, p2, RT, k1, p2—37 sts.
Row 2: K2, p3, k2, p1, k2, p5, k3, p1, k3, p5, k2, p1, k2, p3, k2.
Row 3: P2, k1, LT, p2, k1, p2, RT, k1, LT, p3, k1, p3, RT, k1, LT, p2, k1, p2, RT, k1, p2.
Rows 4-9: Rep Rows 2 and 3 three times.
Row 10: (WS) K2, p1, k2, p5, k2, p1, k3, p5, k3, p1, k2, p5, k2, p1, k2.
Row 11 *inc row:* P2, k1, p2, RT, k1, LT, p2, k1, p3, m1-p/L, RT, k1, LT, m1-p/L, p3, k1, p2, RT, k1, LT, p2, k1, p2—39 sts.
Row 12: K2, p1, k2, p5, k2, p1, k4, p5, k4, p1, k2, p5, k2, p1, k2.
Row 13: P2, k1, p2, RT, k1, LT, p2, k1, p4, RT, k1, LT, p4, k1, p2, RT, k1, LT, p2, k1, p2.
Rows 14-19: Rep Rows 12 and 13 three times.
Row 20: (WS) K2, p3, k2, p1, k2, p5, k4, p1, k4, p5, k2, p1, k2, p3, k2.
Row 21 *inc row:* P2, k1, LT, p2, k1, p2, RT, k1, LT, p4, m1-p/L, k1, m1-p/L, p4, RT, k1, LT, p2, k1, p2, RT, k1, p2—41 sts.
Row 22: K2, p3, k2, p1, k2, p5, k5, p1, k5, p5, k2, p1, k2, p3, k2.
Row 23: P2, k1, LT, p2, k1, p2, RT, k1, LT, p5, k1, p5, RT, k1, LT, p2, k1, p2, RT, k1, p2.
Rows 24-29: Rep Rows 22 and 23 three times.
Row 30: (WS) K2, p1, k2, p5, k2, p1, k5, p5, k5, p1, k2, p5, k2, p1, k2.
Row 31 *inc row:* P2, k1, p2, RT, k1, LT, p2, k1, p5, m1-p/L, RT, k1, LT, m1-p/L, p5, k1, p2, RT, k1, LT, p2, k1, p2—43 sts.
Row 32: K2, p1, k2, p5, k2, p1, k6, p5, k6, p1, k2, p5, k2, p1, k2.
Row 33: P2, k1, p2, RT, k1, LT, p2, k1, p6, RT, k1, LT, p6, k1, p2, RT, k1, LT, p2, k1, p2.
Rows 34-39: Rep Rows 32 and 33 three times.
Row 40: (WS) K2, p3, k2, p1, k2, p5, k6, p1, k6, p5, k2, p1, k2, p3, k2.
Row 41 *inc row:* P2, k1, LT, p2, m1-p/L, k1, p2, RT, k1, LT, p6, k1, p6, RT, k1, LT, p2, k1,m1-p/L, p2, RT, k1, p2—45 sts.
Row 42: K2, p3, k3, p1, k2, p5, k6, p1, k6, p5, k2, p1, k3, p3, k2.
Row 43: P2, k1, LT, p3, k1, p2, RT, k1, LT, p6, k1, p6, RT, k1, LT, p2, k1, p3, RT, k1, p2.
Rows 44-49: Rep Rows 42 and 43 three times.
Row 50: (WS) K2, p1, k3, p5, k2, p1, k6, p5, k6, p1, k2, p5, k3, p1, k2.
Row 51 *inc row:* P2, k1, m1-p/L, p3, RT, k1, LT, p2, k1, p6, RT, k1, LT, p6, k1, p2, RT, k1, LT, p3, m1-p/L, k1, p2—47 sts.
Row 52: K2, p1, k4, p5, k2, p1, k6, p5, k6, p1, k2, p5, k4, p1, k2.
Row 53: P2, k1, p4, RT, k1, LT, p2, k1, p6, RT, k1, LT, p6, k1, p2, RT, k1, LT, p4, k1, p2.
Rows 54-59: Rep Rows 52 and 53 three times.
Row 60: (WS) K2, p3, k4, p1, k2, p5, k6, p1, k6, p5, k2, p1, k4, p3, k2.

Notes

Pullover is worked in the round from the bottom up. Front and back are separated at underarm. At underarm stitches are added at each edge to extend bodice. Then back and front are worked flat to the shoulders. Shoulders are shaped with short rows, then joined with WS together using an exposed three-needle bind off. Sleeves stitches are picked up around the armhole and knitted in the round to the cuff. Neck band is picked up around the neck edge then bound off.

pullover

With larger circ and using the long-tail cast on, CO 142 (158, 174, 190, 206, 222, 238, 254, 270, 286) sts. Place marker (pm) for beg of rnd (BOR) and join to work in the rnd, careful not to twist sts.

Begin stockinette and panel set up

First rnd: *K18 (22, 26, 30, 34, 38, 42, 46, 50, 54), pm for panel, work Rnd 1 of Austrian block panel set up over 35 sts, pm for panel, k18 (22, 26, 30, 34, 38, 42, 46, 50, 54), pm for side; rep from * one more time to end (BOR counts as second side marker).
Work Rnds 2-4 of panel setup.

Begin block panel

Next rnd: *Knit to m, sl m, work Rnd 1 of Austrian block panel to next m, sl m, knit to side m; rep from * one more time to end.
Work Rnds 2-20 of panel, then rep Rnds 1-20 of panel 1 (1, 1, 1, 2, 2, 2, 2, 2, 1) more time(s), then work to Rnd 14 (12, 8, 8, 6, 6, 4, 4, 2, 18) one more time.

Pc meas approx 9¾ (9¼, 8¾, 8¾, 11¾, 11¾, 11¼, 11¼, 11, 10¼)" [25 (23.5, 22, 22, 30, 30, 28.5, 28.5, 28, 26) cm] from beg.

Begin underarm shaping

Next rnd *inc rnd:* *K1, M1L, knit to m, sl m, work next rnd of panel, sl m, knit to 1 st before side m, M1L, k1; rep from * one more time to end (4 sts inc'd)—146 (162, 178, 194, 210, 226, 242, 258, 274, 290) sts.

Next rnd: Work even in patts.

Rep the last 2 rnds one more time—150 (166, 182, 198, 214, 230, 246, 262, 278, 294) sts. Last rnd worked is Rnd 18 (16, 12, 12, 10, 10, 8, 8, 6, 2) of panel.

Separate front and back

Next row *cast on row:* (RS) Using the cable cast on, CO 8 (8, 8, 4, 4, 4, 2, 2, 2, 2) sts, knit to panel m, sl m, work Row 19 (17, 13, 13, 11, 11, 9, 9, 7, 3) of panel to next m, sl m, knit to side m, remove m, then place rem 75 (83, 91, 99, 107, 115, 123, 131, 139, 147) sts onto waste yarn for back.

Front

Next row *cast on row:* (WS) Using the cable cast on, CO 8 (8, 8, 4, 4, 4, 2, 2, 2, 2) sts, purl to m, sl m, work next WS row of panel to next m, sl m, purl to end—91 (99, 107, 107, 115, 123, 127, 135, 143, 151) sts.

Work 0 (2, 6, 6, 8, 8, 10, 10, 12, 16) rows even, ending after Row 20. Work Rows 1-20 of panel one more time, then work to Row 16 one more time.

Pc meas approx 6¼ (6¾, 7¼, 7¼, 7¾, 7¾, 8, 8, 8¼, 9)" [16 (17, 18.5, 18.5, 19.5, 19.5, 20.5, 20.5, 21, 23) cm] from underarm.

Place a locking st marker for neck on either side of center 9 sts.

Begin shoulder shaping

Note: Do not count yarnovers as stitches.

Next row *short row 1:* (RS) Work in est patts to last 3 sts, turn; (WS) yo, work in est patts to last 3 sts, turn.

Begin neck shaping and cont shoulder shaping

Next row *short row 2:* (RS) Yo, work to 2 (2, 2, 2, 2, 2, 3, 3, 3, 3) sts before last gap, turn; (WS) yo, work to neck m, remove m, join new ball of yarn and BO all sts to next m, removing m to BO last st, work to 2 (2, 2, 2, 2, 2, 3, 3, 3, 3) sts before last gap, turn—41 (45, 49, 49, 53, 57, 59, 63, 67, 71) sts rem for each side.

Next row *short row 3:* (RS) Yo, knit to 2 sts before panel m, k2tog, sl m, work to 2 sts before left neck edge, ssk; on right neck edge, k2tog, work to panel m, sl m, ssk, knit to 2 (2, 2, 2, 2, 2, 3, 3, 3, 3) sts before last gap, turn; (WS) yo, work to 2 sts before neck edge, p2tog; then ssp, work to 2 (2, 2, 2, 2, 2, 3, 3, 3, 3) sts before last gap, turn—38 (42, 46, 46, 50, 54, 56, 60, 64, 68) sts rem each side.

Next row *short row 4:* (RS) Yo, knit to 2 sts before panel m, k2tog, sl m, work to neck edge; then work to panel m, sl m, ssk, knit to 2 (2, 2, 2, 2, 2, 3, 3, 3, 3) sts before last gap, turn; (WS) yo, work to neck edge; then work to 2 (2, 2, 2, 2, 2, 3, 3, 3, 3) sts before last gap, turn—37 (41, 45, 45, 49, 53, 55, 59, 63, 67) sts each side.

Rep *short row four* 3 (3, 3, 3, 2, 1, 1, 1, 3, 3) more time(s)—34 (38, 42, 42, 47, 52, 54, 58, 60, 64) sts each side.

Next row *short row 5:* (RS) Yo, knit to 2 sts before panel m, k2tog, sl m, work to neck edge; then work to panel m, sl m, ssk, knit to 2 (2, 3, 3, 3, 3, 3, 3, 4, 4) sts before last gap, turn; (WS) yo, work to neck edge; then work to 2 (2, 3, 3, 3, 3, 3, 3, 4, 4) sts before last gap, turn—33 (37, 41, 41, 46, 51, 53, 57, 59, 63) sts each side.

Rep *short row five* 0 (0, 0, 0, 1, 2, 2, 2, 0, 0) more time(s)—33 (37, 41, 41, 45, 49, 51, 55, 59, 63) sts each side.

Next row *short row 6:* (RS) Yo, work to neck edge; then work to 2 (2, 3, 3, 3, 3, 3, 3, 4, 4) sts before last gap; (WS) yo, work to neck edge; then work to 2 (2, 3, 3, 3, 3, 3, 3, 4, 4) sts before last gap.

Rep *short row six* 2 (2, 2, 2, 3, 0, 2, 2, 5, 6) more times.

Next row *short row 7:* (RS) Yo, work to neck edge; then work to 2 (4, 4, 4, 4, 4, 4, 4, 4, 4) sts before last gap, turn; (WS) yo, work to neck edge; then work to 2 (4, 4, 4, 4, 4, 4, 4, 4, 4) sts before last gap.

Rep *short row seven* 1 (1, 1, 1, 1, 4, 2, 3, 0, 0) more time(s).

Resolve short rows

Next row: (RS) Yo, work to left neck edge, turn; (WS) work to end, working ssp or ssk in pattern to join each yarnover with the st after gap. Break yarn at left neck edge.

Next row: (RS) On right neck edge, work to end, working k2tog or p2tog in pattern to join each yarnover with the st after gap. Break yarn. Place sts onto waste yarn.

Back

Return sts held for back to larger circ.

Next row *pick up row:* (RS) With RS of back facing and beg at right armhole edge, pick up and knit 8 (8, 8, 4, 4, 4, 2, 2, 2, 2) sts in CO sts for right front underarm, knit to panel m, sl m, work Row 19 (17, 13, 13, 11, 11, 9, 9, 7, 3) of panel to next m, sl m, knit to end, then pick up and knit 8 (8, 8, 4, 4, 4, 2, 2, 2, 2) sts in CO sts for left front underarm—91 (99, 107, 107, 115, 123, 127, 135, 143, 151) sts.

Next row: (WS) Purl to panel m, sl m, work next WS row of panel to next m, sl m, purl to end.

Cont in patts for 10 (12, 16, 16, 18, 18, 20, 20, 22, 26) more rows, ending after Row 10 of panel.

Begin increase panel

Note: As stitches in panel are increased, stitches are decreased in stockinette to maintain stitch count.

Next row *inc/dec row:* (RS) Knit to 2 sts before m, k2tog, sl m, work Row 1 of increase panel to next m, sl m, ssk, knit to end.

Cont in St st and work Rows 2-10 of increase panel.

Next row *inc/dec row:* (RS) Knit to 2 sts before m, k2tog, sl m, work next row of increase panel to next m, sl m, ssk, knit to end.

Cont as est, working *inc/dec row* on each inc row of increase panel to Row 26 of panel.

Begin shoulder shaping

Note: Continue to work *inc/dec row* on each inc row in increase panel throughout short row shaping.

Next row *short row 1:* (RS) Work to last 3 sts, turn; (WS) yo, work to last 3 sts, turn.

Next row *short row 2:* (RS) Yo, work to 2 (2, 2, 2, 2, 2, 3, 3, 3, 3) sts before last gap, turn; (WS) yo, work to 2 (2, 2, 2, 2, 2, 3, 3, 3, 3) sts before last gap, turn.

Rep *short row two* 8 (8, 5, 5, 4, 3, 8, 8, 4, 4) more times.

Next row *short row 3:* (RS) Yo, work to 2 (2, 3, 3, 3, 3, 3, 3, 3, 3) sts before last gap, turn; (WS) yo, work to 2 (2, 3, 3, 3, 3, 3, 3, 3, 3) sts before last gap, turn.

Rep *short row three* 0 (0, 3, 3, 5, 3, 0, 0, 0, 0) more times.

Next row *short row 4:* (RS) Yo, work to 2 (4, 4, 4, 4, 4, 4, 4, 4, 4) sts before last gap, turn; (WS) yo, work to 2 (4, 4, 4, 4, 4, 4, 4, 4, 4) sts before last gap, turn.

Rep *short row four* 0 (0, 0, 0, 0, 3, 1, 2, 6, 7) more time(s).

Place a locking st marker for neck on each side of center 25 sts.

Begin neck shaping

Next row *short row 5:* (RS) Yo, work to 2 (4, 4, 4, 4, 4, 4, 4, 4, 4) sts before last gap, turn; (WS) yo, work to neck m, join a new ball of yarn and BO all sts to next m, removing marker to BO last st, work to 2 (4, 4, 4, 4, 4, 4, 4, 4, 4) sts before last gap, turn—33 (37, 41, 41, 45, 49, 51, 55, 59, 63) sts rem for each side.

Resolve short rows

Next row: (RS) Yo, work to right neck edge, turn; (WS) work in patts to end, working ssk or ssp in pattern to join each each yarnover with the st after gap. Break yarn at right shoulder leaving a tail roughly five times the width of the shoulder for finishing.

Next row: (RS) On left shoulder, work in patts to end, working k2tog or p2tog to join each yarnover with the st after gap. Do not break yarn.

Join shoulders

Place sts held for front shoulders onto smaller circ. With RS of pcs held tog and attached yarn, using the three-needle bind off, BO all left shoulder sts. With long tail at right armhole edge, rep for right shoulder.

Gently steam block piece.

Sleeves

With RS facing and larger dpns, beg at underarm, pick up and knit 24 (26, 28, 28, 29, 29, 30, 30, 31, 34) sts to shoulder seam (approx 2 sts for every 3 rows), then pick up and knit 24 (26, 28, 28, 29, 29, 30, 30, 31, 34) sts to underarm—48 (52, 56, 56, 58, 58, 60, 60, 62, 68) sts on needles. Pm for BOR.

First rnd: Knit.

Cont in St st until pc meas 2½" [6.5 cm] from pick-up.

Begin sleeve shaping

Next rnd *dec rnd:* K2, k2tog, knit to last 4 sts, ssk, k2 (2 sts dec'd)—46 (50, 54, 54, 56, 56, 58, 58, 60, 66) sts rem.

Rep *dec rnd* every 14 (14, 14, 14, 12, 12, 10, 10, 10, 6) rows 3 (3, 3, 3, 4, 4, 5, 5, 5, 8) times—40 (44, 48, 48, 48, 48, 48, 48, 50, 50) sts rem.

Cont in St st until sleeve meas 16½ (16½, 16½, 15½, 15½, 15½, 14½, 14½, 14, 14)" [42 (42, 42, 39.5, 39.5, 39.5, 37, 37, 35.5, 35.5) cm] from pick-up.

Next rnd: Bind off purlwise.

Finishing

Weave in ends. Gently steam to block.

Neck trim

With RS facing, smaller size circ, and starting at right shoulder, pick up and knit 1 st in each BO st and 2 sts for every 3 rows around neck edge.

First rnd: Bind off purlwise.

Weave in remaining ends and gently steam neckband.

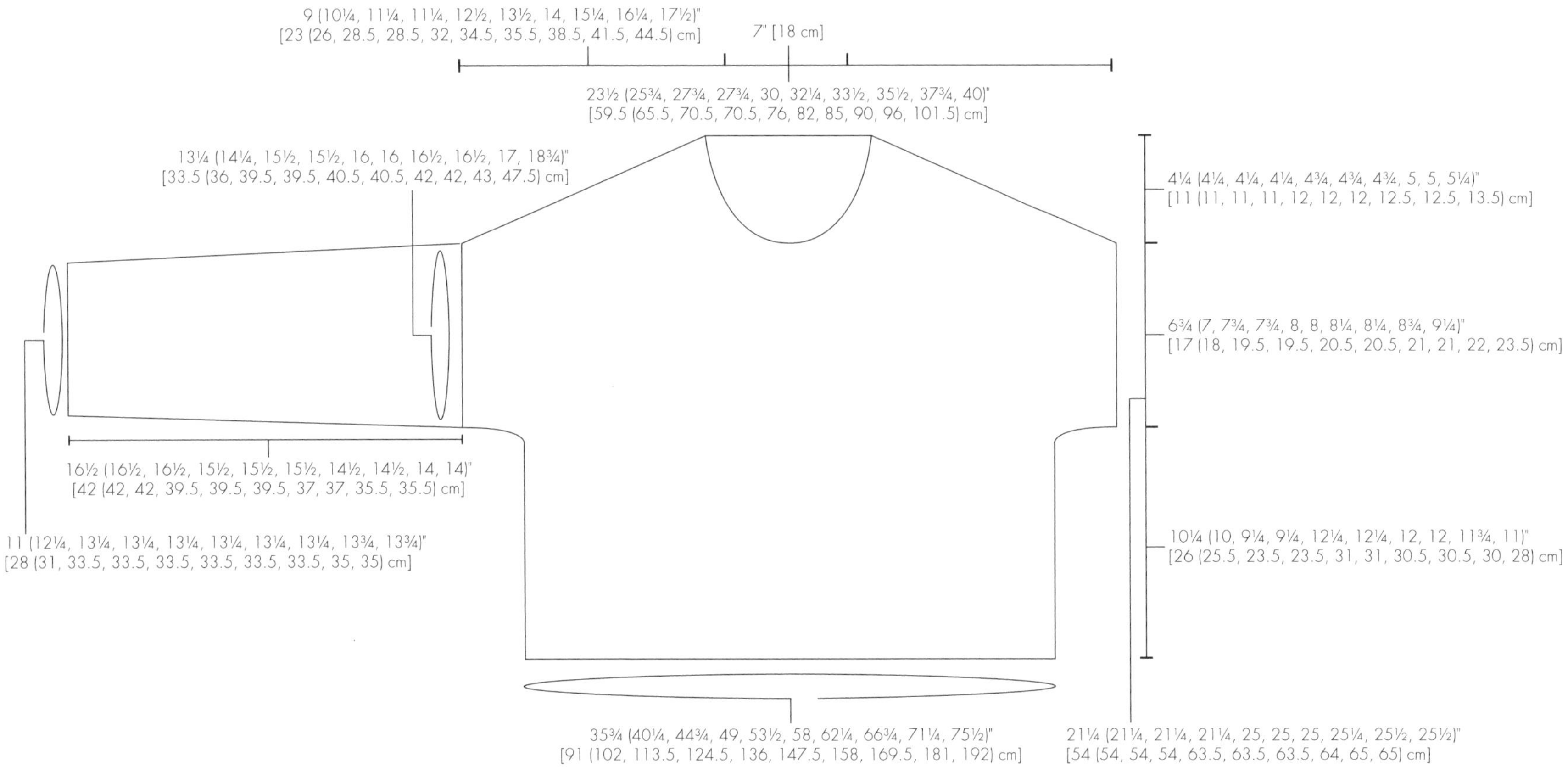

Increase panel

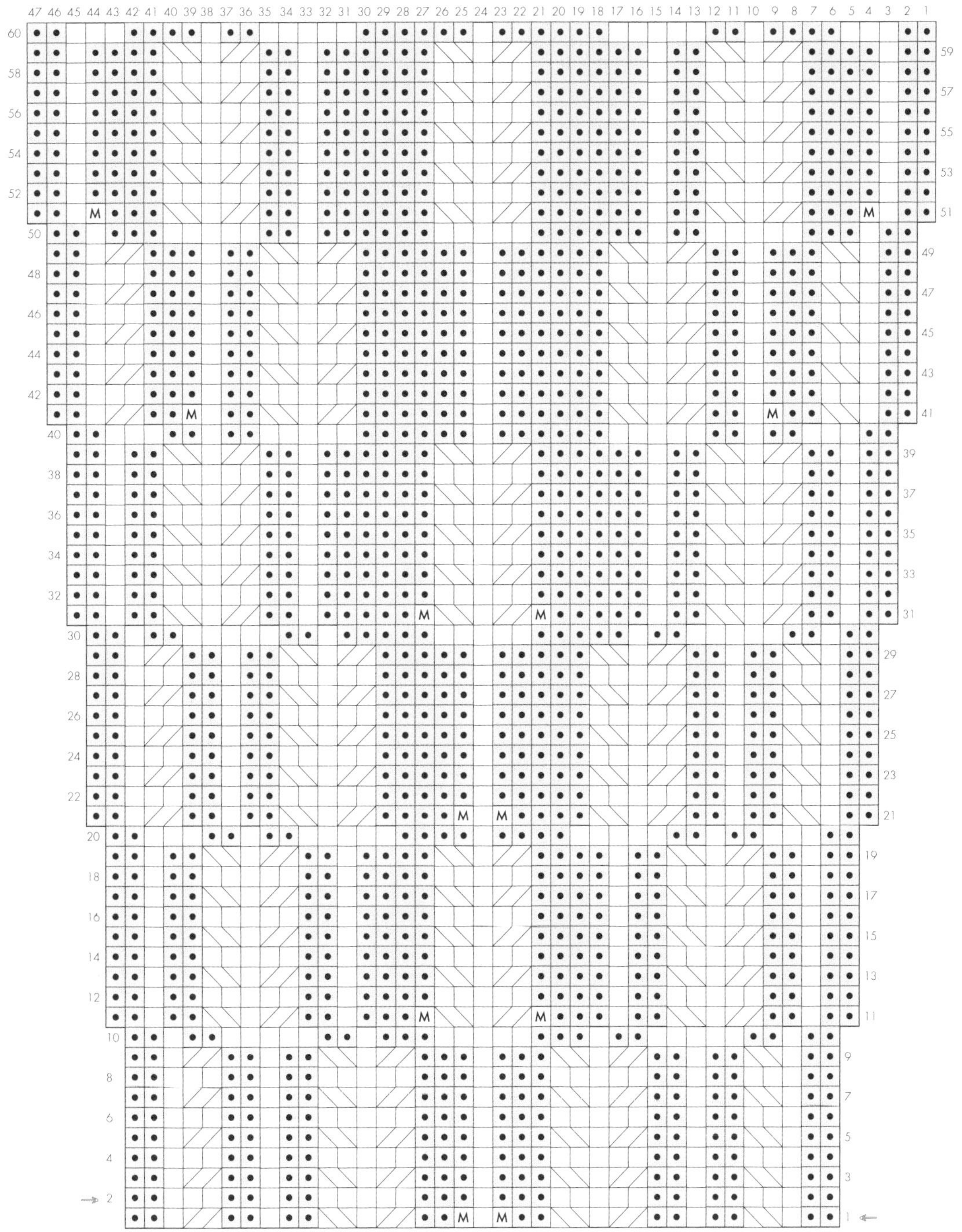

Key

- knit on RS, purl on WS
- • purl on RS, knit on WS
- M m1-p/L
- RT
- LT

Austrian block panel

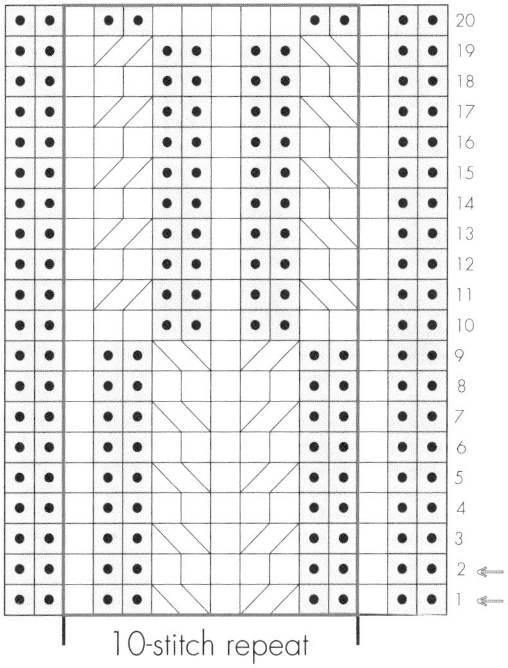

Austrian block setup

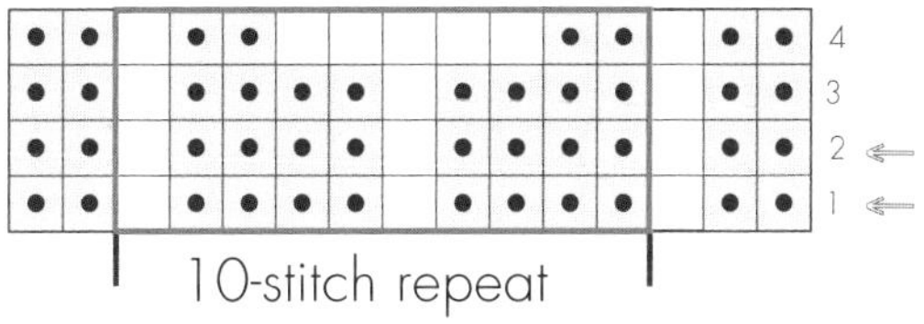

hobblebush

A pared-down classic round-yoke sweater. Without ribbed cuff or hem, the sweater hangs straight and easy. I like colorwork on neutral colors, the rich, bold colors here stand out against plain gray. But because of the chunky scale of the motifs, you could easily work with colors that don't contrast so strongly with each other for a more subtle approach.

Finished measurements
31 (35, 39, 43, 47, 51, 55, 59, 63, 67, 71, 75)" [78.5 (89, 99, 109, 119.5, 129.5, 139.5, 150, 160, 170, 180.5, 190.5) cm] bust circumference; shown in size 39" [99 cm] on a 31" [79 cm], 5'11" [180 cm] model (8" [20.5 cm] positive ease)

Yarn
Owl by Quince & Co
(50% American wool, 50% alpaca; 120yd [110m]/50g)

- 6 (7, 7, 8, 9, 9, 10, 11, 12, 12, 13, 14) skeins Bubo 332 (A)
- 1 skein Allagash 371 (B)
- 1 skein Snowy 300 (C)
- 1 skein Barred 307 (D)
- 1 skein Steppe 327 (E)

Needles

- One 32" circular needle (circ) in size US 10 [6 mm]
- One 16" circ in size US 10 [6 mm]
- One set double-pointed needles in size US 10 [6 mm]

Or size to obtain gauge

Notions

- Stitch markers
- Waste yarn
- Tapestry needle

Gauge
16 sts and 24 rnds = 4" [10 cm] in stockinette stitch, after light steam blocking.

Notes

1. Body is knitted in the round from the bottom up to underarm. Stitches are held for underarm, then more stitches are cast on for sleeves using waste yarn. Yoke is continued in color/stitch patterns to neck edge. Sleeve stitches are picked up from waste yarn cast on and knitted in the round to the cuff.
2. When picking up live stitches from the bottom edge of cast on, you will have one more stitch than the number you cast on. See page 114 for an illustrated tutorial.

> Cast on methods abound. But we're partial to the long-tail cast on, and that's why, for most pieces, we specify using it. It's not a tight cast on, but it's stable. It isn't a loose cast on, so, in a sweater like Hobblebush that has no ribbing or other non-curling edge stitch, it lies nicely flat, once steamed.

pullover

With A, longer circular needle (circ), and using the long-tail cast on, CO 124 (140, 156, 172, 188, 204, 220, 236, 252, 268, 284, 300) sts. Place marker (pm) for beginning of rnd (BOR) and join to work in the rnd, careful not to twist sts.

Begin at bottom edge

First rnd *place markers:* K62 (70, 78, 86, 94, 102, 110, 118, 126, 134, 142, 150), pm for side, k62 (70, 78, 86, 94, 102, 110, 118, 126, 134, 142, 150) to end (BOR counts as second side marker).

Cont in St st until pc meas 14 (14, 14, 14, 14½, 14½, 14½, 15, 15, 15, 15½, 15½)" [35.5 (35.5, 35.5, 35.5, 37, 37, 37, 38, 38, 38, 39.5, 39.5) cm] from beg.

Separate front and back

Next rnd: *Knit to side m, remove m, k6 (6, 6, 8, 8, 8, 8, 10, 12, 12, 12, 14), then place last 12 (12, 12, 16, 16, 16, 16, 20, 24, 24, 24, 28) sts onto waste yarn; rep from * one more time—50 (58, 66, 70, 78, 86, 94, 98, 102, 110, 118, 122) sts rem each for front and back.

Begin yoke

Next rnd *cast on rnd:* K25 (29, 33, 35, 39, 43, 47, 49, 51, 55, 59, 61), pm for new BOR (center back), k25 (29, 33, 35, 39, 43, 47, 49, 51, 55, 59, 61), turn work, with waste yarn make slipknot (first sleeve st), place onto RH needle and using the backward loop cast on, CO 33 (37, 39, 39, 43, 45, 49, 49, 51, 53, 55, 55) more sts for sleeve, turn work, with A, knit across sts cast on for sleeve, knit across front sts, turn work, with waste yarn, make slipknot (first sleeve st), place onto RH needle, and using the backward loop cast on, CO 33 (37, 39, 39, 43, 45, 49, 49, 51, 53, 55, 55) more sts for second sleeve, turn work, with A, knit across sts cast on for sleeve, knit to BOR—168 (192, 212, 220, 244, 264, 288, 296, 308, 328, 348, 356) sts on needle.

Next rnd *place markers:* K25 (29, 33, 35, 39, 43, 47, 49, 51, 55, 59, 61), pm, k34 (38, 40, 40, 44, 46, 50, 50, 52, 54, 56, 56), pm, k50 (58, 66, 70, 78, 86, 94, 98, 102, 110, 118, 122), pm, k34 (38, 40, 40, 44, 46, 50, 50, 52, 54, 56, 56), pm, k25 (29, 33, 35, 39, 43, 47, 49, 51, 55, 59, 61) to end.

With A, knit 0 (0, 2, 4, 6, 8, 10, 12, 12, 14, 14, 16) more rnds.

Begin raglan shaping

Next rnd *dec rnd:* *Knit to 3 sts before m, ssk, k1, sl m, k1, k2tog; rep from * three more times, knit to end (8 sts dec'd)—160 (184, 204, 212, 236, 256, 280, 288, 300, 320, 340, 348) sts rem.

Rep *dec rnd* every 2 rnds 0 (0, 0, 1, 1, 2, 2, 3, 3, 4, 4, 5) more time(s)—160 (184, 204, 204, 228, 240, 264, 264, 276, 288, 308, 308) sts rem. Pc meas approx ½ (½, ¾, 1½, 1¾, 2½, 2¾, 3½, 3½, 4¼, 4¼, 4¾)" [1.5 (1.5, 2, 4, 4.5, 6.5, 7, 9, 9, 11, 11, 12) cm] from underarm.

Begin colorwork and round yoke shaping

Note: Change to shorter circ when necessary.

Next rnd: Work Rnd 1 of Chart 1, removing all markers except BOR as you go.

Work Rnds 2-10 of Chart 1.

Next rnd: With A, knit.

Next rnd *dec rnd:* K1(0, 2, 2, 1, 0, 2, 2, 2, 1, 0, 0), [k2tog, k4 (5, 4, 4, 5, 5, 4, 4, 4, 3, 4, 4)] 26 (26, 33, 33, 32, 34, 43, 43, 45, 57, 51, 51) times, k2tog, k1 (0, 2, 2, 1, 0, 2, 2, 2, 0, 0, 0); 27 (27, 34, 34, 33, 35, 44, 44, 46, 58, 52, 52) sts dec'd—133 (157, 170, 170, 195, 205, 220, 220, 230, 230, 256, 256) sts rem.

Next rnd *dec rnd:* [K2tog, k131 (155, 83, 83, 63, 203, 53, 53, 113, 113, 62, 62)] 1 (1, 2, 2, 3, 1, 4, 4, 2, 2, 4, 4) time(s) to end; 1 (1, 2, 2, 3, 1, 4, 4, 2, 2, 4, 4) st(s) dec'd—132 (156, 168, 168, 192, 204, 216, 216, 228, 228, 252, 252) sts rem.

Next rnd: Work Rnd 1 of Chart 2.

Next rnd: Work Rnd 2 of Chart 2.

Next 3 rnds: With A, knit.

Next rnd *dec rnd:* Work Rnd 1 of Chart 3; 22 (26, 28, 28, 32, 34, 36, 36, 38, 38, 42, 42) sts dec'd—110 (130, 140, 140, 160, 170, 180, 180, 190, 190, 210, 210) sts rem.

Work Rnds 2-9 of Chart 3.

Next rnd *dec rnd:* Work Rnd 10 of chart; 22 (26, 28, 28, 32, 34, 36, 36, 38, 38, 42, 42) sts dec'd—88 (104, 112, 112, 128, 136, 144, 144, 152, 152, 168, 168) sts rem.

Next 2 rnds: With A, knit.

Next rnd: Work Rnd 1 of Chart 4.

Next rnd: Work Rnd 2 of Chart 4.

Next 2 rnds: With A, knit.

Next rnd *dec rnd:* With A, *k2, k2tog; rep from * to end; 22 (26, 28, 28, 32, 34, 36, 36, 38, 38, 42, 42) sts dec'd—66 (78, 84, 84, 96, 102, 108, 108, 114, 114, 126, 126) sts rem.

Next rnd: Work Rnd 1 of Chart 5 to end.

Work Rnds 2-6 of Chart 5.

Begin short row back neck shaping

Note: Do not count yarnovers as stitches.

Next row *short row 1:* With A, k26 (29, 31, 31, 35, 37, 39, 39, 41, 41, 44, 44), turn; (WS) yo, p52 (58, 62, 62, 70, 74, 78, 78, 82, 82, 88, 88), turn.

Next row *short row 2:* (RS) Yo, knit to 6 sts before last gap, turn; (WS) yo, purl to 6 sts before last gap, turn.

Rep *short row 2* one more time.

Next row: (RS) Yo, knit to BOR.

Resolve short rows

Next rnd: With A, knit to yo, k2tog the yo with the st after gap, (k5, k2tog the yo with the st after gap) two times, knit to 1 st before next yo, ssk next st with yo after gap, (k5, ssk next st with yo after gap) two times, knit to end.

Size 31" [78.5 cm] only:

Next rnd *dec rnd:* *K9, k2tog; rep from * to end (6 sts dec'd)—60 sts rem.

Proceed to All sizes.

Size 35" [89 cm] only:

Next rnd *dec rnd:* K3, *k2, k2tog; rep from * to last 3 sts, k3 (18 sts dec'd)—60 sts rem.

Proceed to All sizes.

Sizes - (-, 39, 43, -, -, -, -, -, -, -, -)" [- (-, 99, 109, -, -, -, -, -, -, -, -) cm] only:

Next rnd *dec rnd:* *K1, k2tog, k2, k2tog; rep from * to end (24 sts dec'd)—60 sts rem.

Proceed to All sizes.

Sizes - (-, -, -, 47, 51, 55, 59, 63, 67, 71, 75)" [- (-, -, -, 109, 119.5, 129.5, 139.5, 150, 160, 170, 180.5, 190.5) cm] only:

Next rnd *dec rnd:* *K1, k2tog; rep from * to end; - (-, -, -, 32, 34, 36, 36, 38, 38, 42, 42) sts dec'd— - (-, -, -, 64, 68, 72, 72, 76, 76, 84, 84) sts rem.

All sizes

60 (60, 60, 60, 64, 68, 72, 72, 76, 76, 84, 84) sts on needle.

Next rnd: Bind off all sts purlwise.

Sleeves

With A, RS facing, and double-pointed needles, place first 6 (6, 6, 8, 8, 8, 8, 10, 12, 12, 12, 14) sts held for underarm onto needles, pm for BOR, place rem 6 (6, 6, 8, 8, 8, 8, 10, 12, 12, 12, 14) underarm sts onto needle, then, working one st at a time, pick out waste yarn from sleeve cast on and place each st onto needle, sl 6 (6, 6, 8, 8, 8, 8, 10, 12, 12, 12, 14) underarm sts to RH needle—46 (50, 52, 56, 60, 62, 66, 70, 76, 78, 80, 84) sts on needles.

First rnd: Knit.

Cont in St st for 3 more rnds.

Begin sleeve shaping

Next rnd *dec rnd:* K2, k2tog, knit to last 4 sts, ssk, k2 (2 sts dec'd)—44 (48, 50, 54, 58, 60, 64, 68, 74, 76, 78, 82) sts rem.

Rep *dec rnd* every 18 (14, 10, 10, 8, 8, 8, 6, 6, 6, 6, 6) rnds 4 (5, 6, 7, 8, 9, 10, 11, 12, 13, 14, 15) more times—36 (38, 38, 40, 42, 42, 44, 46, 50, 50, 50, 52) sts rem.

Cont in St st until sleeve meas 18" [45.5 cm] from underarm.

Next rnd: Bind off all sts purlwise.

Finishing

Weave in ends. Steam lightly to maintain texture.

Key

- knit with specified color
- purl with specified color
- k2tog with specified color
- with A, work as specified
- with B, work as specified
- with C, work as specified
- with D, work as specified
- with E, work as specified

Chart 1

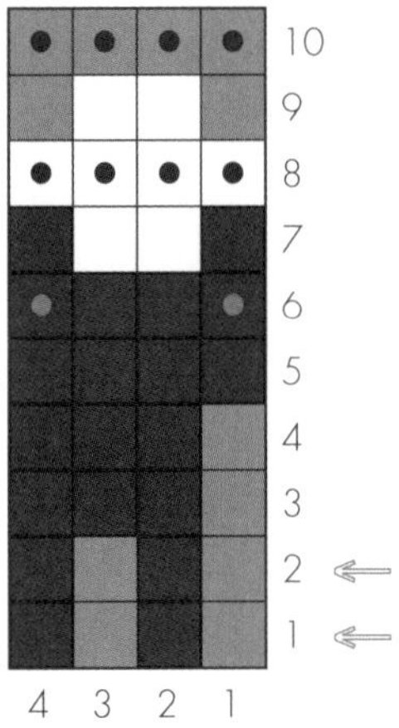

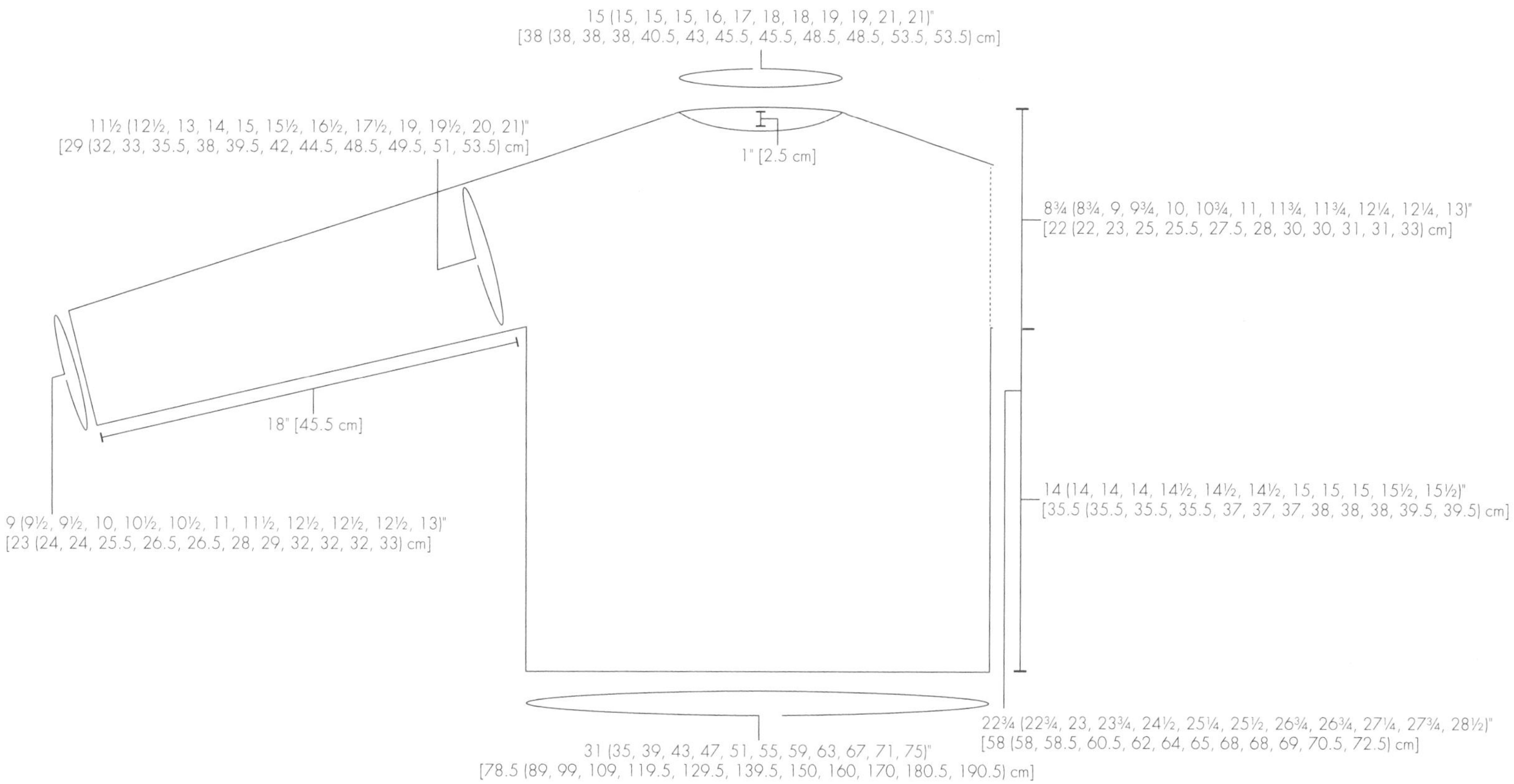

Chart 2

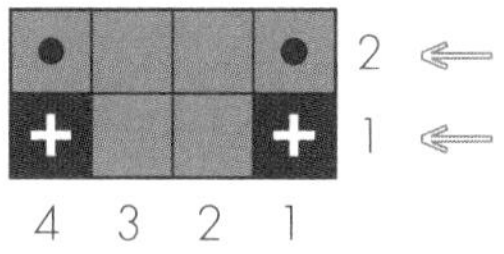

Chart 3

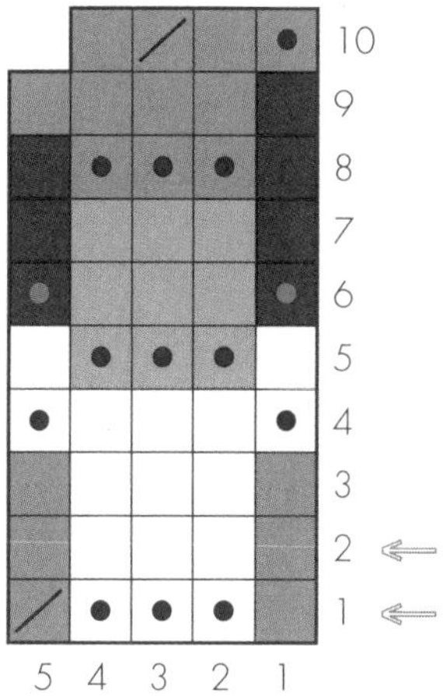

Chart 4

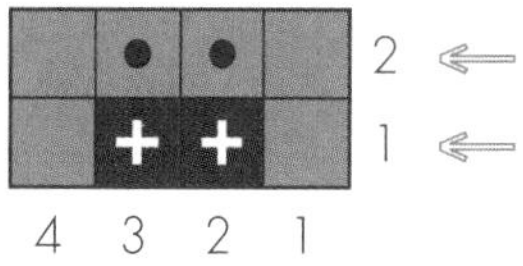

Chart 5

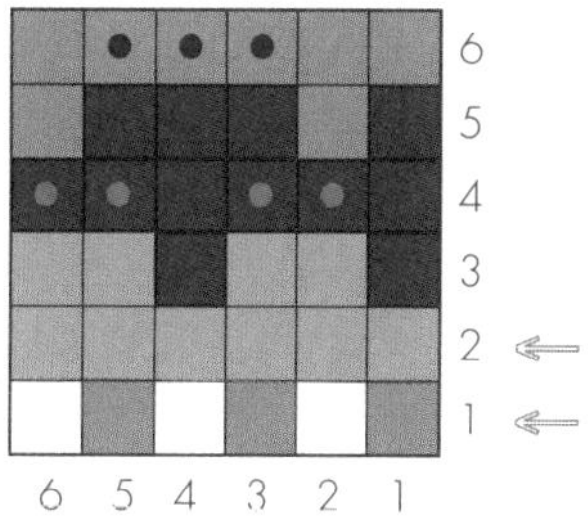

winterberry

This short pullover is a riff on the classic Scandinavian pullover. This version is wide and swingy with a contrast color strip on the ribbed borders. The rib pattern is worked with garter stitch instead of purls between the knitted columns to prevent pulling in. If you want a longer sweater, work more rounds between bottom border and yoke.

Finished measurements
34 (39½, 45¼, 50¾, 56½, 62, 67¾, 73½)" [86.5 (100.5, 115, 129, 143.5, 157.5, 172, 186.5) cm] bust circumference; shown in size 45¼" [115 cm] on a 31" [79 cm], 5'11" [180 cm] tall model (14¼" [36 cm] positive ease)

Yarn
Owl by Quince & Co
(50% American wool, 50% alpaca; 120yd [110m]/50g)
- 6 (6, 7, 8, 9, 10, 12, 14) skeins Barents Sea 326 (A)
- 3 (3, 3, 4, 4, 4, 5, 5) skeins Elf 303 (B)
- 1 skein Steppe 327 (C)

Note: Only approx 20-30 yds of color C are used. If you have Owl leftovers, use them!

Needles
- One 16" circular needle (circ) in size US 8 [5 mm]
- One 32" circ in size US 8 [5 mm]
- One 32" circ in size US 10 [6 mm]
- One spare circ in size US 10 [6 mm]
- One set double-pointed needles (dpns) in size US 10 [6 mm]

Or size to obtain gauge

Notions
- Stitch markers
- Waste yarn
- Tapestry needle

Gauge
17 sts and 22 rnds = 4" [10 cm] in Chart 2 pattern with larger needle, after blocking.

Notes
1. Pullover is knitted in the round from the bottom up to underarm, then front and back are separated and worked flat to the shoulders. Shoulders are shaped with short rows, then joined using the three-needle bind off. For sleeves, stitches are picked up around the armhole and worked in the round to cuff. Neck band is picked up around the neck edge and worked in ribbing.
2. Here is a video link with great tips for working stranded knitting flat: **www.youtube.com/watch?v=Wf9a46CEBO4**

pullover

With B, smaller, longer circular needle (circ), and using the long-tail cast on, CO 150 (175, 200, 225, 250, 275, 300, 325) sts. Place marker (pm) for beg of rnd (BOR) and join to work in the rnd, careful not to twist sts.

Begin garter rib
Rnd 1: P1, *k3, p2; rep from * to last 3 sts, k3, p1.
Rnd 2: Knit.
Cont in est rib for 2" [5 cm], ending after Rnd 1.
Next rnd: With C, work Rnd 2 of rib patt.
Next rnd: With B, work Rnd 1.
Next rnd: With B, work Rnd 2.
Next rnd: With C, work Rnd 1.
With B, cont in garter rib for 4 more rnds, ending after Rnd 1.

Begin stockinette
Next rnd *dec rnd:* With B, *k2tog, k23; rep from * to end; 6 (7, 8, 9, 10, 11, 12, 13) sts dec'd—144 (168, 192, 216, 240, 264, 288, 312) sts rem.
Change to larger circ.

Begin colorwork patts
See colorwork charts, page 92.
Next rnd *place markers:* Work Rnd 1 of Chart 1 for 72 (84, 96, 108, 120, 132, 144, 156) sts, pm for side, work Rnd 1 of chart to end.
Work Rnds 2-7 of Chart 1.
Next rnd: Work Rnd 1 of Chart 2.
Work Rnds 2-6 of Chart 2.
Cont repeating Rnds 1-6 of Chart 2 until pc meas approx 10 (10, 10, 11, 11, 12, 13, 14)" [25.5 (25.5, 25.5, 28, 28, 30.5, 33, 35.5) cm] from beg, ending after Rnd 3.

Begin underarm shaping
Next rnd *inc rnd:* *With A, k1, M1L, knit to 1 st before side marker, M1L, k1, sl m; rep from * one more time (4 sts inc'd)—148 (172, 196, 220, 244, 268, 292, 316) sts.
Next rnd: With A, knit to end.
Next rnd: *With A, k1, then work Rnd 6 of Chart 2 to 1 st before side m, with A, k1, sl m; rep from * one more time.

Separate front and back
Next rnd *cast on rnd:* With A and using the cable cast on, CO 5 sts, knit to side m, then place rem sts for front onto waste yarn.

Back
Note: Read RS rows from right to left and WS rows from left to right.
Next row: (WS) Using the cable cast on, CO 5 sts, purl to end—84 (96, 108, 120, 132, 144, 156, 168) sts on needle.
Next row: (RS) Work Row 3 of Chart 2 to end.
Cont working back and forth in Chart 2 as est, for 1 (1, 1, 7, 7, 7, 13, 13) more row(s), ending after Row 4.

Begin yoke charts
Next row: (RS) Work Row 1 of Chart 3.
Work Rows 2-5 of Chart 3.
Next row *inc row:* (WS) With A, p1, m1-p/L, purl to end (1 st inc'd)—85 (97, 109, 121, 133, 145, 157, 169) sts.
Next row: (RS) Beg with stitch 3 (5, 7, 1, 3, 5, 7, 1) of chart, work Row 1 of Chart 4, ending with stitch 7 (5, 3, 1, 7, 5, 3, 1) of chart.
Next row: (WS) Beg with stitch 7 (5, 3, 1, 7, 5, 3, 1) of chart, work back across Row 2 of Chart 4, ending with stitch 3 (5, 7, 1, 3, 5, 7, 1) of chart.
Work Rows 3-7 of Chart 4.
Next row *dec row:* (WS) With A, p1, p2tog, purl to end (1 st dec'd)—84 (96, 108, 120, 132, 144, 156, 168) sts rem.
Next row: (RS) Work Row 1 of Chart 5.
Work Rows 2-5 of Chart 5.
Next row *inc row:* (WS) With A, p1, m1-p/L, purl to end (1 st inc'd)—85 (97, 109, 121, 133, 145, 157, 169) sts.
Next row: (RS) Beg with stitch 5 (7, 1, 3, 5, 7, 1, 3) of chart, work Row 1 of Chart 6, ending with stitch 1 (7, 5, 3, 1, 7, 5, 3) of chart.
Next row: (WS) Beg with stitch 1 (7, 5, 3, 1, 7, 5, 3) of chart, work back across Row 2 of Chart 6, ending with stitch 5 (7, 1, 3, 5, 7, 1, 3) of chart.
Work Rows 3-9 of Chart 6.

Set up shoulder shaping
Note: Chart 2 for shoulders begins with Row 1 on the WS; read RS rows from right to left and WS rows from left to right.
Next row *place markers:* (WS) Working Row 1 of Chart 2, p30 (35, 40, 46, 51, 56, 62, 67), pm for neck, p25 (27, 29, 29, 31, 33, 33, 35), pm for neck, p30 (35, 40, 46, 51, 56, 62, 67) sts to end.
Cont in Chart 2 as est for 2 (2, 4, 4, 6, 8, 8, 10) more rows, ending after a WS row.
Pc meas meas approx 6½ (6½, 7, 8, 8¼, 8¾, 9¾, 10¼)" [16.5 (16.5, 18, 20.5, 21, 22, 25, 26) cm] from underarm.

Begin shoulder shaping

Note: Do not count yarnovers as stitches. Maintain stitch pattern as best you can while working short rows.

Next row *short row 1:* (RS) Work in Chart 2 as est to last 4 (4, 5, 6, 6, 7, 7, 8) sts, turn; (WS) yo, work in Chart 2 as est to last 4 (4, 5, 6, 6, 7, 7, 8) sts, turn.

Next row *short row 2:* (RS) Yo, work in est patts to 4 (5, 5, 6, 7, 8, 9, 10) sts before last gap, turn; (WS) yo, work in est patts to 4 (5, 5, 6, 7, 8, 9, 10) sts before last gap, turn.

Next row *short row 3:* (RS) Yo, work to 4 (5, 6, 7, 8, 9, 10, 11) sts before last gap, turn; (WS) yo, work to 4 (5, 6, 7, 8, 9, 10, 11) sts before last gap, turn.

Rep *short row 3* two more times.

Begin neck shaping

Next row *short row 4:* (RS) Yo, work to 4 (5, 6, 7, 8, 9, 10, 11) sts before last gap, turn; (WS) yo, work to neck m, remove m, BO all sts to next m, removing m to BO last st, then purl to 4 (5, 6, 7, 8, 9, 10, 11) sts before gap, turn—30 (35, 40, 46, 51, 56, 62, 67) sts rem for each side.

Resolve short rows

Next row: (RS) Yo, work in patt to neck edge, turn.

Next row: (WS) Purl to end, working ssp to join each yo with the st after gap.

Break yarn. Join yarn at left neck edge, ready to work a RS row.

Next row: (RS) Knit all sts, working k2tog to join each yo with the st after gap.

Break yarn.

Front

Return sts held for front to longer circ.

Next row *pick up row:* (RS) With RS of front facing and beg at left armhole edge, with A, pick up and knit 5 sts in underarm CO from left back, knit to end, then pick up and knit 5 sts in underarm CO from right back—84 (96, 108, 120, 132, 144, 156, 168) sts on needle.

Next row: (WS) With A, purl to end.

Next row: (RS) Work Row 3 of Chart 2.

Cont working back and forth in Chart 2 as est, for 1 (1, 1, 7, 7, 7, 13, 13) more row(s), ending after Row 4.

Begin yoke charts

Next row: (RS) Work Row 1 of Chart 3.

Work Rows 2-5 of Chart 3.

Next row *inc row:* (WS) With A, p1, m1-p, purl to end (1 st inc'd)—85 (97, 109, 121, 133, 145, 157, 169) sts.

Next row: (RS) Beg with stitch 3 (5, 7, 1, 3, 5, 7, 1) of chart, work Row 1 of Chart 4, ending with stitch 7 (5, 3, 1, 7, 5, 3, 1) of chart.

Next row: (WS) Beg with stitch 7 (5, 3, 1, 7, 5, 3, 1) of chart, work back across Row 2 of Chart 4, ending with stitch 3 (5, 7, 1, 3, 5, 7, 1) of chart.

Work Rows 3-7 of Chart 4.

Next row *dec row:* (WS) With A, p1, p2tog, purl to end (1 st dec'd)—84 (96, 108, 120, 132, 144, 156, 168) sts rem.

Next row: (RS) Work Row 1 of Chart 5.

Work Rows 2-5 of Chart 5.

Next row *inc row:* (WS) With A, p1, m1-p/L, purl to end (1 st inc'd)—85 (97, 109, 121, 133, 145, 157, 169) sts.

Next row: (RS) Beg with stitch 5 (7, 1, 3, 5, 7, 1, 3) of chart, work Row 1 of Chart 6, ending with stitch 1 (7, 5, 3, 1, 7, 5, 3) of chart.

Next row: (WS) Beg with stitch 1 (7, 5, 3, 1, 7, 5, 3) of chart, work back across Row 2 of Chart 6, ending with stitch 5 (7, 1, 3, 5, 7, 1, 3) of chart.

Next row: Work Row 3 of Chart 6 as est.

Next row *place markers:* (WS) With A, p38 (44, 50, 56, 62, 68, 74, 80), pm for neck, p9, pm for neck, p38 (44, 50, 56, 62, 68, 74, 80) sts to end.

Begin neck shaping

Next row: (RS) With A, knit to m, remove m, join a new ball of A and BO all sts to next m, removing m to BO last st, knit to end—38 (44, 50, 56, 62, 68, 74, 80) sts rem for each side.

Next row: (WS) Join a new ball of B and work Row 6 of Chart 6 to right neck edge; on left neck edge, BO 2 (3, 3, 3, 3, 3, 3, 3) sts, then work Chart 6 as est to end.

Next row: (RS) Work Row 7 of Chart 6 to left neck edge; then BO 2 (3, 3, 3, 3, 3, 3, 3) sts, work in Row 7 of Chart 6 to end—36 (41, 47, 53, 59, 65, 71, 77) sts each side.

Next row: (WS) Work in Chart 6 as est to right neck edge; then BO 2 sts, work to end.

Next row: (RS) Work in Chart 6 as est to left neck edge; then BO 2 sts, work to end—34 (39, 45, 51, 57, 63, 69, 75) sts each side.

Next row: (WS) Work Row 1 of Chart 2 to right neck edge; then BO 2 sts, work Row 1 of Chart 2 to end.

Next row: (RS) Work Row 2 of Chart 2 to left neck edge; then BO 2 sts, work Row 2 of Chart 2 to end—32 (37, 43, 49, 55, 61, 67, 73) sts each side.

Next row: (WS) Work Chart 2 as est to right neck edge; then work Chart 2 as est to end.

Sizes 34 (39½, -, -, -, -, -, -)" [86.5 (100.5, -, -, -, -, -, -) cm] only:
Proceed to Begin shoulder shaping.

Sizes - (-, 45¼, 50¾, 56½, 62, 67¾, 73½)" [- (-, 115, 129, 143.5, 157.5, 172, 186.5) cm] only:
Next row *dec row:* (RS) Work next row of Chart 2 to 2 sts before left neck edge, ssk; then k2tog, work chart to end— - (-, 42, 48, 54, 60, 66, 72) sts each side.
Next row: (WS) Work next row of Chart 2 to right neck edge; then work chart to end.
Rep the last 2 rows - (-, 0, 0, 1, 2, 2, 3) more time(s)— - (-, 42, 48, 53, 58, 64, 69) sts each side.

Begin shoulder shaping

Note: Do not count yarnovers as stitches. Maintain stitch pattern as best you can while working short rows.
Next row *short row 1:* (RS) Work next row of Chart 2 to 2 sts before left neck edge, ssk; then k2tog, work Chart 2 to last 4 (4, 5, 6, 6, 7, 7, 8) sts, turn; (WS) yo, work to right neck edge; then work to last 4 (4, 5, 6, 6, 7, 7, 8) sts, turn—31 (36, 41, 47, 52, 57, 63, 68) sts each side.
Next row *short row 2:* (RS) Yo, work to 2 sts before left neck edge, ssk; then k2tog, work to 4 (5, 5, 6, 7, 8, 9, 10) sts before last gap, turn; (WS) yo, work to right neck edge; then work to 4 (5, 5, 6, 7, 8, 9, 10) sts before last gap, turn—30 (35, 40, 46, 51, 56, 62, 67) sts each side.
Next row *short row 3:* (RS) Yo, work to left neck edge; then work to 4 (5, 6, 7, 8, 9, 10, 11) sts before last gap, turn; (WS) yo, work to right neck edge; then work to 4 (5, 6, 7, 8, 9, 10, 11) sts before last gap, turn.
Rep *short row 3* three more times.

Resolve short rows

Next row: (RS) Yo, work to left neck edge, turn.
Next row: (WS) Purl to end, working ssp to join each yo with the st after the gap. Break A, leaving a long tail for finishing. Join yarn at right neck edge, ready to work a RS row.
Next row: (RS) Knit to end, working k2tog to join each yo with the st after the gap.
Do not break A.

Join shoulders

Place sts held for back shoulders onto spare circ. With RS of pcs held tog and attached yarn, using the three-needle bind off, BO all right shoulder sts. With long tail at left armhole edge, rep for left shoulder.
Gently steam block piece.

Sleeves

With RS facing, A, and double-pointed needles (dpns), beg at underarm, pick up and knit 30 (30, 32, 36, 38, 40, 44, 46) sts to shoulder seam (approx 4 sts for every 5 rows), then pick up and knit 30 (30, 32, 36, 38, 40, 44, 46) sts to underarm—60 (60, 64, 72, 76, 80, 88, 92) sts on needles. Pm for BOR.

Begin colorwork

First rnd: Work Rnd 1 of Chart 2 to end.
Cont in Chart 2 until sleeve meas 1¾" [4.5 cm] from pick-up.

Begin sleeve shaping

Next rnd *dec rnd:* K1, k2tog, work next rnd of Chart 2 to last 3 sts, ssk, k1—58 (58, 62, 70, 74, 78, 86, 90) sts rem.
Rep *dec rnd* every 6 (14, 9, 6, 8, 6, 5, 6) rnds 9 (4, 6, 10, 7, 9, 13, 10) more times—40 (50, 50, 50, 60, 60, 60, 70) sts rem.
Cont in Chart 2 until pc meas approx 15" [38 cm] from pick-up, ending after Rnd 2 or 5.
Next rnd: Beg on stitch 2 of chart, work Rnd 1 of Chart 1, ending with stitch 1 (3, 3, 3, 1, 1, 1, 3) of chart.

Begin garter rib cuff

Rnd 1: K1, *p2, k3; rep from * to last 4 sts, p2, k2.
Rnd 2: Knit.
Rep Rnd 1 one more time.
Next rnd: With C, work Rnd 2.
Next rnd: With B, work Rnd 1.
Next rnd: With C, work Rnd 2.
With B, cont in garter rib until cuff meas 2¾" [7 cm], ending after Rnd 2.
Next rnd: Bind off in pattern.

Finishing

Weave in ends. Lightly steam- or wet-block to finished measurements.

Neck band

With RS facing, B, and smaller, shorter circ, beg at right shoulder seam, pick up and knit 1 st in each BO st and 1 st in each row around neck edge, making sure to pick up a number divisible by 4. Pm for BOR.

Begin rib

Rnd 1: P1, *k2, p2; rep from * to last 3 sts, k2, p1.
Rnd 2: Knit.
Rep Rnds 1 and 2 three times.
Next rnd: Bind off in pattern.

Weave in ends. Lightly steam neck band.

Chart 1

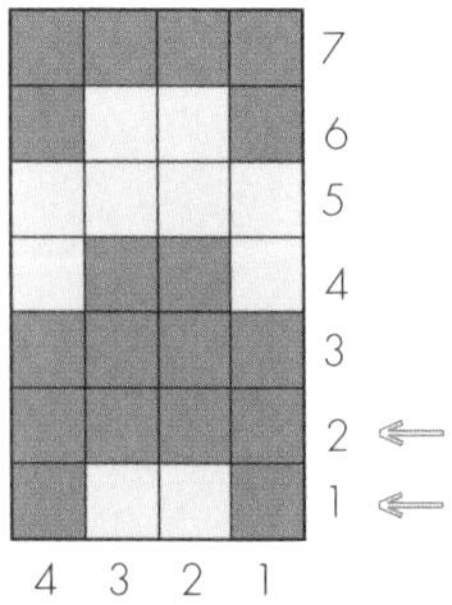

Chart 2

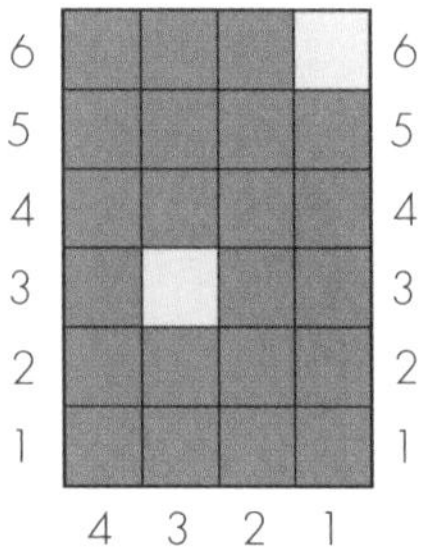

Chart 3

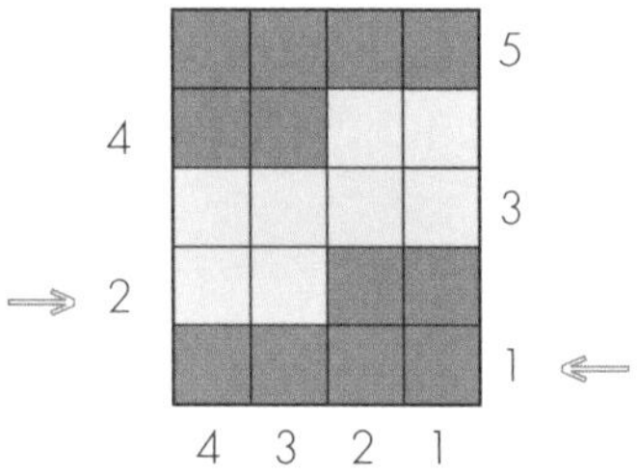

Chart 4

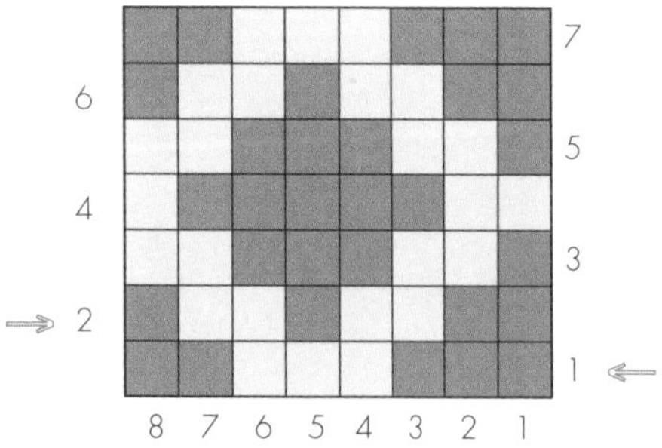

Chart 5

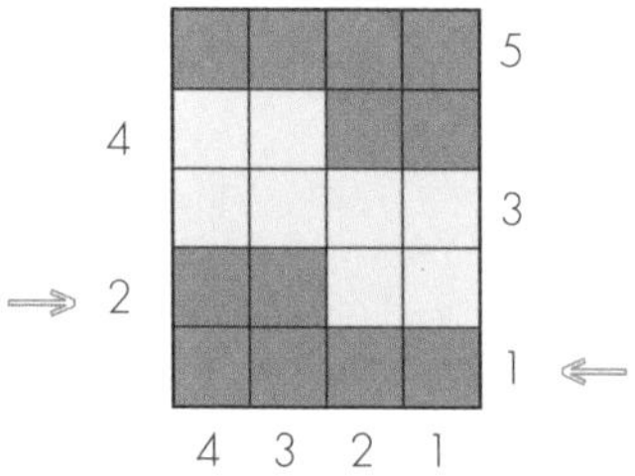

Chart 6

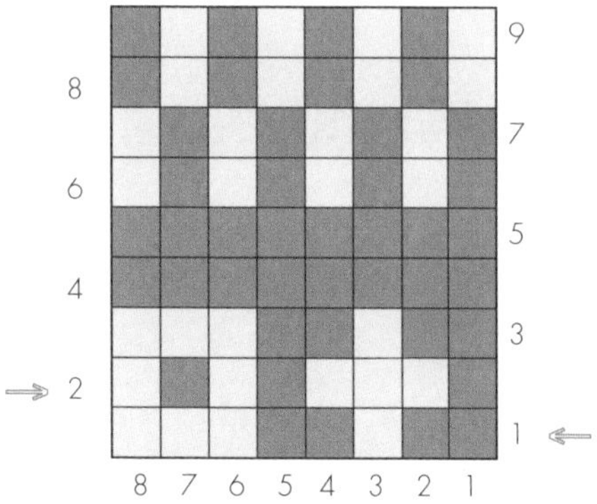

Key

with A, knit on RS, purl on WS

with B, knit on RS, purl on WS

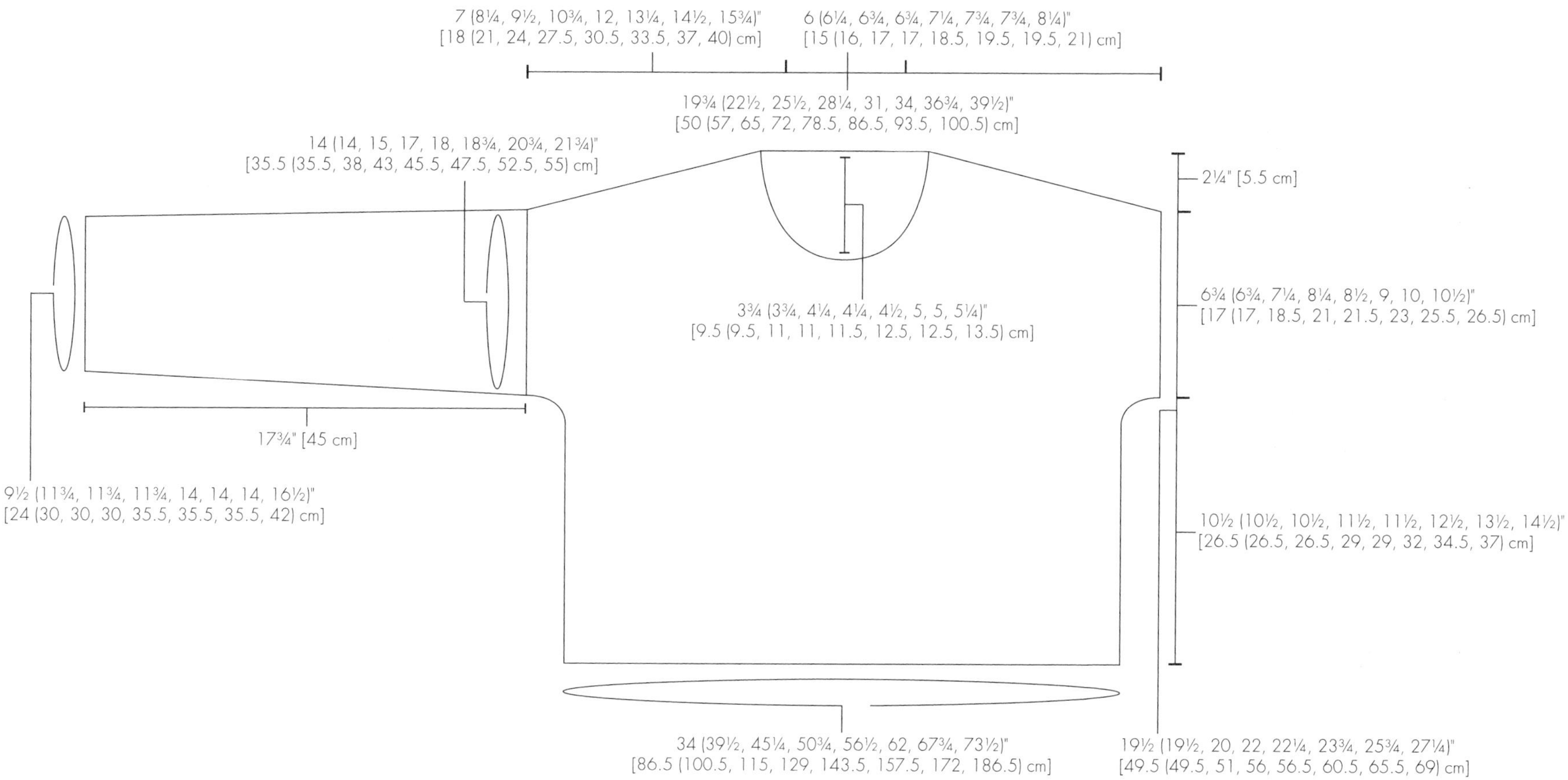

7 (8¼, 9½, 10¾, 12, 13¼, 14½, 15¾)"
[18 (21, 24, 27.5, 30.5, 33.5, 37, 40) cm]
6 (6¼, 6¾, 6¾, 7¼, 7¾, 7¾, 8¼)"
[15 (16, 17, 17, 18.5, 19.5, 19.5, 21) cm]
19¾ (22½, 25½, 28¼, 31, 34, 36¾, 39½)"
[50 (57, 65, 72, 78.5, 86.5, 93.5, 100.5) cm]
14 (14, 15, 17, 18, 18¾, 20¾, 21¾)"
[35.5 (35.5, 38, 43, 45.5, 47.5, 52.5, 55) cm]
2¼" [5.5 cm]
3¾ (3¾, 4¼, 4¼, 4½, 5, 5, 5¼)"
[9.5 (9.5, 11, 11, 11.5, 12.5, 12.5, 13.5) cm]
6¾ (6¾, 7¼, 8¼, 8½, 9, 10, 10½)"
[17 (17, 18.5, 21, 21.5, 23, 25.5, 26.5) cm]
17¾" [45 cm]
9½ (11¾, 11¾, 11¾, 14, 14, 14, 16½)"
[24 (30, 30, 30, 35.5, 35.5, 35.5, 42) cm]
10½ (10½, 10½, 11½, 11½, 12½, 13½, 14½)"
[26.5 (26.5, 26.5, 29, 29, 32, 34.5, 37) cm]
34 (39½, 45¼, 50¾, 56½, 62, 67¾, 73½)"
[86.5 (100.5, 115, 129, 143.5, 157.5, 172, 186.5) cm]
19½ (19½, 20, 22, 22¼, 23¾, 25¾, 27¼)"
[49.5 (49.5, 51, 56, 56.5, 60.5, 65.5, 69) cm]

witch hazel

This brief little jacket couldn't be simpler. It skims the ribs, hugs the neck, and the sleeves end gently just short of the wrists. The deep, center front borders are worked in a tidy honeycomb stitch at the same time as the rest of the sweater body. The border pattern continues over the shoulders and down the back for a few inches. Other than that, it's plain and simple.

Finished measurements
34 (38, 42, 46, 50, 54, 58, 62, 66, 70, 74, 78)" [86.5 (96.5, 106.5, 117, 127, 137, 147.5, 157.5, 167.5, 178, 188, 198) cm] bust circumference; shown in size 46" [117 cm] on a 31" [79 cm], 5'11" [180 cm] tall model (15" [38 cm] positive ease)

Yarn
Owl by Quince & Co
(50% American wool, 50% alpaca; 120yd [110m]/50g)

- 5 (6, 7, 7, 8, 9, 10, 11, 12, 13, 14, 16) skeins Steppe 327

Needles

- One 32" circular needle (circ) in size US 6 [4 mm]
- One 32" circ in size US 8 [5 mm]
- One spare circ in size US 8 [5 mm]
- One set double-pointed needles (dpns) in size US 6 [4 mm]
- One set dpns in size US 8 [5 mm]

Or size to obtain gauge

Notions

- Stitch markers
- Waste yarn
- Cable needle (optional)
- Tapestry needle

Gauge
16 sts and 25 rows = 4" [10 cm] in stockinette stitch with larger needle, after blocking.

Panel (multiple of 4 stitches + 2)
See also chart, page 98.
Row 1: (RS) P1, *RT, LT; rep from * to last st, p1.
Row 2: K1, purl to last st, k1.
Row 3: P1, *LT, RT; rep from * to last st, p1.
Row 4: K1, purl to last st, k1.
Repeat Rows 1-4 for front panel.

Notes
Jacket is knitted flat from the bottom up, with wide borders at center-front edges. Fronts and back are separated at underarm and worked flat to shoulders with short-row shoulder shaping. Shoulders are joined using the three-needle bind off. Sleeve stitches are picked up around the armhole and knitted in the round to the cuff. Stitches held for right and left collar are worked to center back neck, then are joined using the three-needle bind off and are seamed to back neck.

jacket

With smaller circ and using the long-tail cast on, CO 159 (175, 197, 213, 231, 247, 267, 285, 301, 319, 339, 355) sts. Do not join.

Begin rib and front panels

First row *place markers:* (RS) Work Row 1 of panel over 22 (22, 22, 30, 30, 30, 38, 38, 38, 38, 46, 46) sts, pm, k1, (p1, k1) to last 22 (22, 22, 30, 30, 30, 38, 38, 38, 38, 46, 46) sts, pm, work Row 1 of panel to end.

Next row: Work next row of panel to m, sl m, p1, (k1, p1) to next m, sl m, work next row of panel to end.

Next row: Work next row of panel to m, sl m, k1, (p1, k1) to next m, sl m, work next row of panel to end.

Work 1 more WS row as est.

Change to larger circ.

Begin stockinette and cont front panels

Next row *dec row:* (RS) Work next row of panel to m, sl m, k9 (8, 8, 8, 10, 8, 10, 8, 10, 9, 11, 12), k2tog, [k14 (17, 15, 15, 13, 15, 15, 14, 15, 14, 14, 15), k2tog] 6 (6, 8, 8, 10, 10, 10, 12, 12, 14, 14, 14) times, k8 (7, 7, 7, 9, 7, 9, 7, 9, 8, 10, 11) sts to next m, sl m, work next row of panel to end; 7 (7, 9, 9, 11, 11, 11, 13, 13, 15, 15, 15) sts dec'd—152 (168, 188, 204, 220, 236, 256, 272, 288, 304, 324, 340) sts rem.

Next row: Work panel to m, sl m, purl to next m, sl m, work panel to end.

Next row: Work panel to m, sl m, knit to next m, sl m, work panel to end.

Cont in St st and panels until pc meas approx 7 (7, 7, 7, 8, 8, 8, 8, 9, 9, 9, 10)" [18 (18, 18, 18, 20.5, 20.5, 20.5, 20.5, 23, 23, 23, 25.5) cm] from beg, ending after Row 1 of panels.

Next row *place markers:* (WS) Work panel to m, sl m, p20 (24, 30, 26, 30, 34, 32, 36, 40, 44, 42, 46), pm for side, p68 (76, 84, 92, 100, 108, 116, 124, 132, 140, 148, 156), pm for side, p20 (24, 30, 26, 30, 34, 32, 36, 40, 44, 42, 46) sts to next m, sl m, work panel to end.

Begin underarm shaping

Next row *inc row:* Work in patt to 1 st before side m, M1R, k1, sl m, k1, M1L, knit to 1 st before side m, M1R, k1, sl m, k1, M1L, work in patt to end (4 sts inc'd)—156 (172, 192, 208, 224, 240, 260, 276, 292, 308, 328, 344) sts.

Work 1 WS row. Last row worked is Row 4 of panels.

Separate fronts and back

Next row: (RS) Work in patt to side m, remove m and place next 70 (78, 86, 94, 102, 110, 118, 126, 134, 142, 150, 158) sts onto waste yarn for back, then place rem 43 (47, 53, 57, 61, 65, 71, 75, 79, 83, 89, 93) sts onto separate waste yarn for left front—43 (47, 53, 57, 61, 65, 71, 75, 79, 83, 89, 93) sts rem on needle for right front.

Right front

Next row: (WS) Using the cable cast on, CO 5 sts, work in patt to end—48 (52, 58, 62, 66, 70, 76, 80, 84, 88, 94, 98) sts.

Next row: (RS) Work in patt to end.

Cont in patts until pc meas approx 5¼ (5¾, 6, 6¾, 7, 7¼, 7¼, 8, 8¾, 9, 10, 10¾)" [13.5 (14.5, 15, 17, 18, 18.5, 18.5, 20.5, 22, 23, 25.5, 27.5) cm] from underarm, ending after Row 4 (2, 4, 4, 2, 4, 4, 4, 4, 2, 4, 4) of panel.

Begin shoulder shaping

Note: Do not count yarnovers as stitches.

Next row *short row 1:* (RS) Work in est patts to last 5 (5, 5, 5, 5, 5, 6, 6, 7, 7, 6, 7) sts, turn; (WS) yo, work in est patts to end.

Next row *short row 2:* (RS) Work to 5 (5, 5, 5, 5, 5, 6, 6, 6, 6, 6) sts before last gap, turn; (WS) yo, work to end.

Rep *short row two* 3 (4, 5, 4, 5, 6, 5, 5, 5, 6, 6, 6) times.

Next row *short row 3:* (RS) Work to 6 (5, 6, 7, 6, 5, 7, 5, 8, 6, 5, 8) sts before last gap, turn; (WS) yo, work to end.

Next row *short row 4:* (RS) Work to 8 sts before last gap, turn; (WS) yo, work to end.

Rep *short row four* 0 (0, 0, 1, 1, 1, 2, 2, 2, 2, 3, 3) more time(s).

Resolve short rows and increase row

Next row *inc row:* (RS) Work 9 sts in patt, M1L, then place last 10 sts just worked onto waste yarn for right trim, then maintaining pattern as best you can, k2tog to join each yo with the st after gap to end.

Break yarn, leaving a tail roughly five times the width of the shoulder for finishing. Place rem 39 (43, 49, 53, 57, 61, 67, 71, 75, 79, 85, 89) sts onto waste yarn for shoulder.

Left front

Return sts held for left front to larger circ. Join yarn ready to work a RS row.

Next row: (RS) Using the cable cast on, CO 5 sts, knit to m, work next row of panel to end—48 (52, 58, 62, 66, 70, 76, 80, 84, 88, 94, 98) sts.

Next row: (WS) Work in patt to end.

Cont in patt until pc meas approx 5¼ (5¾, 6, 6¾, 7, 7¼, 7¼, 8, 8¾, 9, 10, 10¾)" [13.5 (14.5, 15, 17, 18, 18.5, 18.5, 20.5, 22, 23, 25.5, 27.5) cm] from underarm, ending after Row 1 (3, 1, 1, 3, 1, 1, 1, 1, 3, 1, 1) of panel.

Begin shoulder shaping

Next row *short row 1:* (WS) Work in est patt to last 5 (5, 5, 5, 5, 5, 6, 6, 7, 7, 6, 7) sts, turn; (RS) yo, work in est patts to end.

Next row *short row 2:* (WS) Work to 5 (5, 5, 5, 5, 5, 5, 6, 6, 6, 6, 6) sts before last gap, turn; (RS) yo, work to end.

Rep *short row two* 3 (4, 5, 4, 5, 6, 5, 5, 5, 6, 6, 6) times.

Next row *short row 3:* (WS) Work to 6 (5, 6, 7, 6, 5, 7, 5, 8, 6, 5, 8) sts before last gap, turn; (RS) yo, work to end.

Next row *short row 4:* (WS) Work to 8 sts before last gap, turn; (RS) yo, work to end.

Rep *short row four* 0 (0, 0, 1, 1, 1, 2, 2, 2, 2, 3, 3) more time(s).

Resolve short rows and increase row

Next row: (WS) Work 9 sts in patt, m1-p/L, place last 10 sts just worked onto waste yarn for left trim, then, maintaining pattern as best you can, ssp to join each yo with the st after gap. Break yarn, leaving a long tail for finishing. Place rem 39 (43, 49, 53, 57, 61, 67, 71, 75, 79, 85, 89) sts onto waste yarn for shoulder.

Back

Return sts held for back to larger circ.

Next row: (RS) With RS of back facing and beg at right armhole edge, pick up and knit 5 sts in underarm CO from right front, knit to end across back sts, then pick up and knit 5 sts in underarm CO from left front—80 (88, 96, 104, 112, 120, 128, 136, 144, 152, 160, 168) sts on needle.

Next row: Purl.

Cont in St st until back meas 3½ (3¾, 4¼, 4¼, 5, 5, 5, 5, 5, 5¾, 6½, 7¼)" [9 (9.5, 11, 11, 12.5, 12.5, 12.5, 12.5, 12.5, 14.5, 16.5, 18.5) cm] from underarm, ending after a RS row.

Next row *inc row:* (WS) P26 (30, 36, 32, 36, 40, 38, 42, 46, 50, 48, 52), pm for panel, p7 (7, 3, 2, 2, 2, 11, 11, 11, 11, 15, 15), [m1-p/L, p1 (1, 1, 2, 2, 2, 1, 1, 1, 1, 1, 1)] 14 (14, 18, 18, 18, 18, 30, 30, 30, 30, 34, 34) times, p7 (7, 3, 2, 2, 2, 11, 11, 11, 11, 15, 15), pm for panel, p26 (30, 36, 32, 36, 40, 38, 42, 46, 50, 48, 52) sts to end; 14 (14, 18, 18, 18, 18, 30, 30, 30, 30, 34, 34) sts inc'd—94 (102, 114, 122, 130, 138, 158, 166, 174, 182, 194, 202) sts.

Begin back panel

Next row: (RS) Knit to m, sl m, work Row 1 of panel to next m, sl m, knit to end.

Next row: Purl to m, sl m, work next row of panel to next m, sl m, purl to end.

Cont as est until Rows 1-4 of panel have been worked a total of 2 (2, 2, 3, 2, 3, 3, 4, 5, 4, 5, 5) times, then work the first 2 (2, 2, 2, 2, 0, 0, 0, 2, 2, 0, 0) rows one more time.

Pc meas approx 5¼ (5¾, 6, 6¾, 7, 7¼, 7¼, 8, 8¾, 9, 10, 10¾)" [13.5 (14.5, 15, 17, 18, 18.5, 18.5, 20.5, 22, 23, 25.5, 27.5) cm] from underarm.

Begin shoulder shaping

Next row *short row 1:* (RS) Work in est patt to last 5 (5, 5, 5, 5, 5, 6, 6, 7, 7, 6, 7) sts, turn; (WS) yo, work in est patt to last 5 (5, 5, 5, 5, 5, 6, 6, 7, 7, 6, 7) sts, turn.

Next row *short row 2:* (RS) Yo, work to 5 (5, 5, 5, 5, 5, 5, 6, 6, 6, 6, 6) sts before last gap, turn; (WS) yo, work to 5 (5, 5, 5, 5, 5, 5, 6, 6, 6, 6, 6) sts before last gap, turn.

Rep *short row two* 3 (4, 5, 4, 5, 6, 5, 5, 5, 6, 6, 6) times.

Next row *short row 3:* (RS) Yo, work to 6 (5, 6, 7, 6, 5, 7, 5, 8, 6, 5, 8) sts before last gap, turn; (WS) yo, work to 6 (5, 6, 7, 6, 5, 7, 5, 8, 6, 5, 8) sts before last gap, turn.

Next row *short row 4:* (RS) Yo, work to 8 sts before last gap, turn; (WS) yo, work to 8 sts before last gap, turn.

Rep *short row four* 0 (0, 0, 1, 1, 1, 2, 2, 2, 2, 3, 3) more time(s).

Next row: (RS) Yo, work in patt to end, working k2tog to join each yo with st after gap. Place a locking st marker on each side of center 16 (16, 16, 16, 16, 16, 24, 24, 24, 24, 24, 24) sts for neck.
Next row: (WS) Work to neck m, remove m, BO all sts to next m, removing marker to BO last st, work to end, working ssp to join each yo with st after gap—39 (43, 49, 53, 57, 61, 67, 71, 75, 79, 85, 89) sts rem for each shoulder.

Next row: (RS) Knit to right neck edge, break yarn, join at left neck edge, knit to end.
Do not break yarn.

Join shoulders

Place sts held for left front onto spare larger circ. With RS of pcs held tog and attached yarn, using the three-needle bind off, BO all sts for left shoulder.
Place sts held for right front onto spare larger circ. With RS of pcs held tog and long tail at right shoulder, using the three-needle bind off, BO all sts for right shoulder.
Gently steam block piece.

Sleeves

With RS facing and larger dpns, beg at center of underarm, pick up and knit 22 (24, 25, 28, 29, 30, 30, 33, 36, 37, 41, 44) sts to shoulder seam (approx 2 sts for every 3 rows), then pick up and knit 22 (24, 25, 28, 29, 30, 30, 33, 36, 37, 41, 44) sts to underarm—44 (48, 50, 56, 58, 60, 60, 66, 72, 74, 82, 88) sts on needles. Pm for BOR.

Begin stockinette

Next rnd: Knit.
Cont in St st for 1" [2.5 cm].

Begin sleeve shaping

Next rnd *dec rnd:* K1, k2tog, knit to last 3 sts, ssk, k1 (2 sts dec'd)—42 (46, 48, 54, 56, 58, 58, 64, 70, 72, 80, 86) sts rem.
Rep *dec rnd* every 12 (12, 10, 8, 8, 8, 8, 6, 6, 6, 4, 4) rnds 2 (2, 2, 4, 1, 1, 1, 4, 2, 1, 9, 8) more time(s), then every 10 (10, 8, 6, 6, 6, 6, 4, 4, 4, 2, 2) rnds 2 (2, 3, 2, 6, 6, 6, 5, 8, 10, 4, 6) times—34 (38, 38, 42, 42, 44, 44, 46, 50, 50, 54, 58) sts rem.
Cont in St st until sleeve meas 10" [25.5 cm] from pick-up.
Change to smaller dpns.

Begin cuff trim

Next rnd: *K1, p1; rep from * to end.
Cont in est rib for 1" [2.5 cm].
Next rnd: Bind off in pattern.

Finishing

Weave in ends. Steam- or wet-block cardi to finished measurements.

Right neck trim

Place a locking stitch marker at center back neck.
Return sts held for right trim to smaller circ or dpn.
Join yarn ready to work a WS row.
Next row: (WS) Purl to last st, k1.
Next row: P1, work in patt to last st, k1.
Cont as est until trim reaches center back neck marker, ending after a RS row. Make note of last row worked.
Break yarn, leaving a long tail for finishing. Place sts onto waste yarn.

Left neck trim

Return sts held for left trim to smaller circ or dpn.
Join yarn ready to work a RS row.
Next row: (RS) K1, work in patt to last st, p1.
Next row: K1, purl to end.
Cont as est until trim reaches center back neck marker, ending after same RS row as right trim.
Break yarn, leaving a long tail for finishing.

Join trim

Place sts held for right trim onto smaller dpn. With RS of pcs held tog and long tail at right trim, using the three-needle bind off, BO all sts.
Seam side of neck trim to back neck using long tails.

Weave in remaining ends. Block again, if you like.

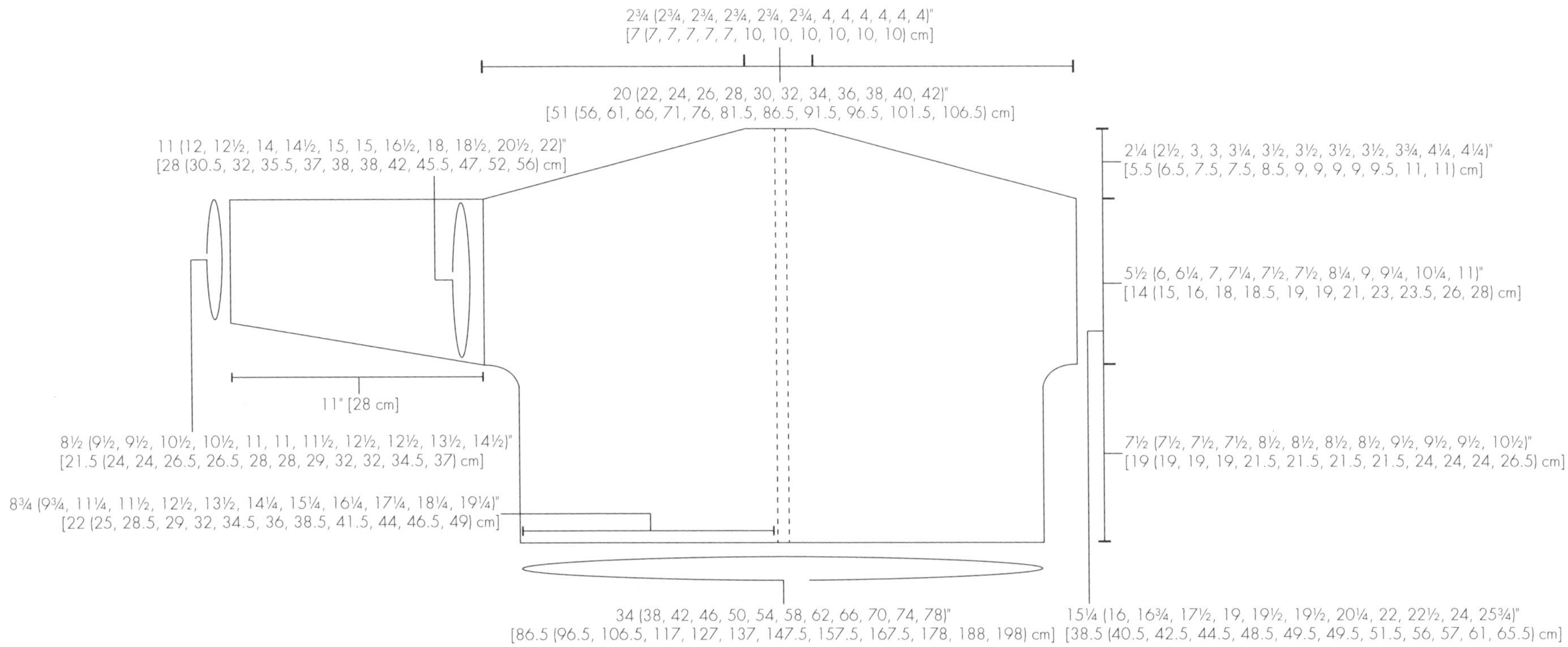

Chart

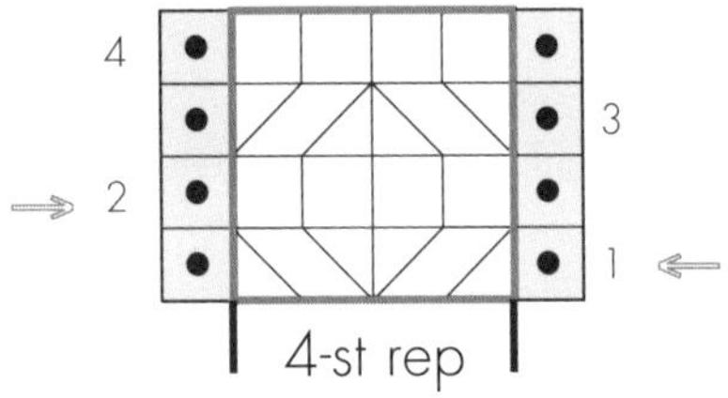

Key

- knit on RS, purl on WS
- purl on RS, knit on WS
- RT
- LT
- pattern repeat

buttonbush

I have a soft spot for anything garter stitch or peplum. This little jacket (think Dickens and fingerless mitts) has gussets worked either side of the waist for hip flare. The sleeves are extra-long and skinny. Back neck of collar, gussets, and sleeves are easily picked up and knitted—garter stitch makes it easy (two rows to one stitch). Only the buttons require sewing. Use a single ply of the working yarn to match the jacket color. I used bone buttons, but pearl-faced ones would be lovely, as would distressed metal or wood to push the vintage feel.

Finished measurements
29 (32, 34, 37, 39, 42, 44, 47, 49, 52, 54, 57, 59, 62)" [73.5 (81.5, 86.5, 94, 99, 106.5, 112, 119.5, 124.5, 132, 137, 145, 150, 157.5) cm] bust circumference; shown in size 32" on a 31" [79 cm], 5'11" [180 cm] tall model (1" [2.5 cm] positive ease)

Yarn
Owl by Quince & Co
(50% American wool, 50% alpaca; 120yd [110m]/50g)
- 9 (10, 11, 11, 12, 13, 14, 15, 16, 17, 17, 19, 19, 21) skeins Allagash 371

Needles
- One 32" circular needle (circ) in size US 9 [5.5 mm]
- One spare circ in size US 9 [5.5 mm]
- One set double-pointed needles in size US 9 [5.5 mm]

Or size to obtain gauge

Notions
- Stitch markers
- Waste yarn
- Tapestry needle
- Locking stitch markers
- 3 (3, 3, 3, 3, 5, 5, 5, 5, 5, 5, 5, 5, 5) buttons, approx 1" [25 mm] diameter

Gauge
16 sts and 32 rows = 4" [10 cm] in garter stitch, after light steam blocking.

Notes
Jacket begins on three separate pieces, back and two fronts. Pieces are joined at the waist and knitted in one piece to the underarm. Collar is worked at same time as an extension of the center front edge. Stitches are added at the armhole to extend the bodice, then fronts and back are separated and worked flat to the shoulders. Shoulders are shaped with short rows then joined with WS together using an exposed three-needle bind off. Sleeves are picked up from around the armhole edge and knitted in the round to the cuff. Right and left collars are continued by joining the stitches with decreases along the back neck and are finished with short row shaping. The collars are joined with the three-needle bind off.

Garter stitch looks the same from RS or WS. To avoid confusion when working this jacket, place a locking stitch marker in a contrasting color on the RS of pieces. You'll always know what's what.

jacket

Begin back
Using the long-tail cast on, CO 26 (28, 32, 34, 38, 40, 44, 46, 50, 52, 56, 58, 62, 64) sts.
First row: (RS) Purl.

Begin garter stitch
Next row: (WS) Knit.
Knit 2 more rows.

Begin side shaping
Next row *inc row:* (RS) K3, M1L, knit to last 3 sts, M1L, k3 (2 sts inc'd)—28 (30, 34, 36, 40, 42, 46, 48, 52, 54, 58, 60, 64, 66) sts.
Cont in garter st and rep *inc row* every 4 rows one more time, then every RS row 9 (11, 11, 13, 13, 15, 15, 17, 17, 19, 19, 21, 21, 23) times—48 (54, 58, 64, 68, 74, 78, 84, 88, 94, 98, 104, 108, 114) sts.
Next row *place markers:* (WS) K12 (13, 14, 16, 17, 18, 19, 21, 22, 23, 24, 26, 27, 29), pm for dart, k24 (28, 30, 32, 34, 38, 40, 42, 44, 48, 50, 52, 54, 56), pm for dart, k12 (13, 14, 16, 17, 18, 19, 21, 22, 23, 24, 26, 27, 29) sts to end.

Begin dart decreases and continue side shaping
Next row *inc/dec row:* (RS) K3, M1L, knit to 2 sts before dart m, k2tog, sl m, k1, ssk, knit to 3 sts before next dart m, k2tog, k1, sl m, ssk, knit to last 3 sts, M1L, k3 (2 sts inc'd and 4 sts dec'd)—46 (52, 56, 62, 66, 72, 76, 82, 86, 92, 96, 102, 106, 112) sts rem.

Continue side shaping
Rep *inc row* every RS row four more times—54 (60, 64, 70, 74, 80, 84, 90, 94, 100, 104, 110, 114, 120) sts.
Next row: (WS) Knit.
Break yarn. Place sts onto waste yarn.

Begin left front
CO 13 (14, 16, 17, 19, 20, 22, 23, 25, 26, 28, 29, 31, 32) sts.
First row: (RS) Purl.

Begin garter stitch
Next row: (WS) Knit.
Knit 2 more rows.

Begin side shaping
Next row *inc row:* (RS) K3, M1L, knit to end (1 st inc'd)—14 (15, 17, 18, 20, 21, 23, 24, 26, 27, 29, 30, 32, 33) sts.
Cont in garter st and rep *inc row* every 4 rows one more time, then every RS row 14 (16, 16, 18, 18, 20, 20, 22, 22, 24, 24, 26, 26, 28) times—29 (32, 34, 37, 39, 42, 44, 47, 49, 52, 54, 57, 59, 62) sts.
Next row: (WS) Knit.
Break yarn. Place sts onto waste yarn.

Begin right front
CO 13 (14, 16, 17, 19, 20, 22, 23, 25, 26, 28, 29, 31, 32) sts.
First row: (RS) Purl.

Begin garter stitch
Next row: (WS) Knit.
Knit 2 more rows.

Begin side shaping
Next row *inc row:* (RS) Knit to last 3 sts, M1L, k3 (1 st inc'd)—14 (15, 17, 18, 20, 21, 23, 24, 26, 27, 29, 30, 32, 33) sts.
Cont in garter st and rep *inc row* every 4 rows one more time, then every RS row 1 (2, 2, 2, 2, 2, 2, 2, 2, 2, 2, 2, 2, 2) time(s)—16 (18, 20, 21, 23, 24, 26, 27, 29, 30, 32, 33, 35, 36) sts.
Next row: (WS) Knit.

Make buttonhole
Next row *inc and buttonhole row 1:* (RS) K3, yo, k2tog, work to last 3 sts, M1L, k3 (1 st inc'd)—17 (19, 21, 22, 24, 25, 27, 28, 30, 31, 33, 34, 36, 37) sts.
Next row *buttonhole row 2:* Knit to yo, knit into yo, k3.
Next row *inc and buttonhole row 3:* K3, knit into yo again, knit to last 3 sts, M1L, k3—18 (20, 22, 23, 25, 26, 28, 29, 31, 32, 34, 35, 37, 38) sts.

Continue side shaping
Rep *inc row* every RS row 9 (10, 10, 12, 12, 6, 6, 7, 7, 8, 8, 9, 9, 10) times—27 (30, 32, 35, 37, 32, 34, 36, 38, 40, 42, 44, 46, 48) sts.
Next row: (WS) Knit.

Sizes 29 (32, 34, 37, 39, -, -, -, -, -, -, -, -, -)" [73.5 (81.5, 86.5, 94, 99, -, -, -, -, -, -, -, -, -) cm] only:
Proceed to All sizes.

Sizes - (-, -, -, -, 42, 44, 47, 49, 52, 54, 57, 59, 62)" [- (-, -, -, -, 112, 119.5, 124.5, 132, 137, 145, 150, 157.5) cm] only:
Rep *buttonhole rows 1-3*— - (-, -, -, -, 34, 36, 38, 40, 42, 44, 46, 48, 50) sts.
Rep *inc row* every RS row - (-, -, -, -, 6, 6, 7, 7, 8, 8, 9, 9, 10) more times— - (-, -, -, -, 40, 42, 45, 47, 50, 52, 55, 57, 60) sts.
Next row: (WS) Knit.

All sizes
Rep *buttonhole rows 1-3*—29 (32, 34, 37, 39, 42, 44, 47, 49, 52, 54, 57, 59, 62) sts.
Next row: (WS) Knit.
Do not break yarn.

Join fronts and back
Next row *joining row:* (RS) With RS of all pcs facing, knit across right front sts, pm for side, return sts held for back to LH needle, knit to 2 sts before first dart m, k2tog, sl m, k1, ssk, knit to 3 sts before next dart m, k2tog, k1, sl m, ssk, knit to end of back, pm for side, return sts held for left front to LH needle and knit to end—108 (120, 128, 140, 148, 160, 168, 180, 188, 200, 208, 220, 228, 240) sts on needle; 29 (32, 34, 37, 39, 42, 44, 47, 49, 52, 54, 57, 59, 62) sts for each front and 50 (56, 60, 66, 70, 76, 80, 86, 90, 96, 100, 106, 110, 116) sts for back.
Next row: (WS) Knit.
Knit 6 (8, 8, 10, 10, 8, 8, 10, 10, 12, 12, 10, 10, 12) more rows, ending after a WS row.

Begin back dart increases
Next row *back inc row:* (RS) Knit to side m, sl m, knit to dart m, M1L, sl m, knit to next dart m, sl m, M1L, knit to end (2 sts inc'd)—110 (122, 130, 142, 150, 162, 170, 182, 190, 202, 210, 222, 230, 242) sts.
Knit 9 (9, 9, 11, 11, 1, 1, 1, 1, 1, 1, 5, 5, 5) row(s), ending after a WS row.

Begin side shaping
Sizes 29 (32, 34, 37, 39, -, -, -, -, -, -, -, -, -)" [73.5 (81.5, 86.5, 94, 99, -, -, -, -, -, -, -, -, -) cm] only:
Next row *inc and buttonhole row 1:* (RS) K3, yo, k2tog, knit to side m, M1L, sl m, knit to dart m, M1L, sl m, knit to next dart m, sl m, M1L, knit to side m, sl m, M1L, knit to end (4 sts inc'd)—114 (126, 134, 146, 154, -, -, -, -, -, -, -, -, -) sts.
Next 2 rows: Work *buttonhole rows 2 and 3*.
Knit 2 rows, ending after a RS row.
Proceed to All sizes.

Sizes - (-, -, -, -, 42, 44, 47, 49, 52, 54, 57, 59, 62)" [- (-, -, -, -, 106.5, 112, 119.5, 124.5, 132, 137, 145, 150, 157.5) cm] only:
Next 3 rows: Work *buttonhole rows 1-3*.
Knit - (-, -, -, -, 9, 9, 11, 11, 13, 13, 9, 9, 9) rows, ending after a WS row.
Next row *side and back inc row:* (RS) Knit to side m, M1L, sl m, knit to dart m, M1L, sl m, knit to next dart m, sl m, M1L, knit to side m, sl m, M1L, knit to end (4 sts inc'd)— - (-, -, -, -, 166, 174, 186, 194, 206, 214, 226, 234, 246) sts.
Knit - (-, -, -, -, 3, 3, 3, 3, 3, 3, 9, 9, 11) rows, ending after a WS row.
Next 3 rows: Rep *buttonhole rows 1-3*.
Knit - (-, -, -, -, 2, 2, 2, 2, 2, 2, 1, 1, 1) row(s).
Rep *side and back inc row* - (-, -, -, -, 0, 0, 0, 0, 0, 0, 1, 1, 1) more time(s)— - (-, -, -, -, 166, 174, 186, 194, 206, 214, 230, 238, 250) sts.

All sizes
Next row *place markers:* (WS) K3, pm for collar, knit to last 3 sts, pm for collar, k3.

Begin collar shaping
Next row *collar inc row:* (RS) Knit to collar m, M1L, sl m, knit to next collar m, sl m, M1L, k3 (2 sts inc'd)—116 (128, 136, 148, 156, 168, 176, 188, 196, 208, 216, 232, 240, 252) sts.
Knit 3 (3, 3, 3, 3, 1, 1, 1, 1, 1, 1, 7, 7, 7) row(s), ending after a WS row.
Rep *side and back inc row* 1 (1, 1, 1, 1, 1, 1, 1, 1, 1, 1, 0, 0, 0) time(s)—120 (132, 140, 152, 160, 172, 180, 192, 200, 212, 220, 232, 240, 252) sts.
Knit 3 (3, 3, 3, 3, 5, 5, 5, 5, 5, 5, 0, 0, 0) rows, ending after a WS row.
Next row: (RS) Rep *collar inc row*—122 (134, 142, 154, 162, 174, 182, 194, 202, 214, 222, 234, 242, 254) sts.
Knit 5 (5, 5, 5, 5, 5, 5, 5, 5, 5, 5, 3, 3, 3) rows, ending after a WS row.
Next row: (RS) Rep *side and back inc row*—126 (138, 146, 158, 166, 178, 186, 198, 206, 218, 226, 238, 246, 258) sts.
Knit 1 (1, 1, 1, 1, 1, 1, 1, 1, 1, 1, 3, 3, 3) row(s).

Next row: (RS) Rep *collar inc row*—128 (140, 148, 160, 168, 180, 188, 200, 208, 220, 228, 240, 248, 260) sts on needle: 35 (38, 40, 43, 45, 48, 50, 53, 55, 58, 60, 63, 65, 68) sts for each front and 58 (64, 68, 74, 78, 84, 88, 94, 98, 104, 108, 114, 118, 124) sts for back.
Knit 7 rows, ending after a WS row.
Pc meas approx 6 (6¼, 6¼, 6¾, 6¾, 7¼, 7¼, 7¾, 7¾, 8¼, 8¼, 8¾, 8¾, 9¼)" [15 (16, 16, 17, 17, 18.5, 18.5, 19.5, 19.5, 21, 21, 22, 22, 23.5) cm] from joining of fronts and back.

Separate fronts and back

Next row *collar inc row:* (RS) Knit to collar m, M1L, remove m, knit to side m, remove m and place sts to next side m onto waste yarn for back, removing back dart markers, remove side m, then place rem sts onto waste yarn for left front, keeping collar m in place.
Place a locking st marker into first st of this row for counting.

Right front

Next row *cast on row:* (WS) Using the cable cast on, CO 5 sts, knit to end—41 (44, 46, 49, 51, 54, 56, 59, 61, 64, 66, 69, 71, 74) sts.
Cont in garter st until pc meas 5¾ (6, 6¼, 6½, 6¾, 7, 7¼, 7½, 7¾, 8, 8¼, 8½, 8¾, 9)" [14.5 (15, 16, 16.5, 17, 18, 18.5, 19, 19.5, 20.5, 21, 21.5, 22, 23) cm] from underarm, ending after a WS row.
Place a locking st marker into first st of this row for counting.

Begin shoulder shaping

Note: Do not count yarnovers as stitches.
Next row *short row 1:* (RS) Knit to last 3 (3, 3, 3, 3, 3, 3, 4, 4, 4, 4, 4, 4, 4) sts, turn; (WS) yo, knit to end.
Next row *short row 2:* (RS) Knit to 2 (2, 2, 2, 2, 2, 2, 3, 3, 3, 3, 3, 3, 3) sts before last gap, turn; (WS) yo, knit to end.
Rep *short row two* 8 (8, 6, 3, 2, 2, 0, 10, 9, 10, 8, 5, 4, 1) more time(s).
Next row *short row 3:* (RS) Knit to 3 (3, 3, 3, 3, 3, 3, 4, 4, 4, 4, 4, 4, 4) sts before last gap, turn; (WS) yo, knit to end.
Rep *short row three* 0 (1, 3, 6, 7, 8, 10, 0, 1, 1, 3, 6, 7, 10) more time(s).

Resolve short rows

Next row: (RS) K17 (17, 17, 17, 18, 18, 18, 18, 19, 19, 19, 19, 20, 20), place sts just worked onto waste yarn for collar, then knit to end, working k2tog to join each yarnover with the st after gap. Break yarn.

Left front

Return sts held for left front to circ. Join yarn ready to work a RS row.
Next row *collar inc and cast on row:* (RS) Using the cable cast on, CO 5 sts, knit to collar m, remove m, M1L, knit to end—41 (44, 46, 49, 51, 54, 56, 59, 61, 64, 66, 69, 71, 74) sts.
Place a locking st marker into first st of this row for counting.
Cont in garter st until left front meas same number of rows as right front between markers for counting, ending after a WS row.
Next row: (RS) Knit.

Begin shoulder shaping

Note: Do not count yarnovers as stitches.
Next row *short row 1:* (WS) Knit to last 3 (3, 3, 3, 3, 3, 3, 4, 4, 4, 4, 4, 4, 4) sts, turn; (RS) yo, knit to end.
Next row *short row 2:* (WS) Knit to 2 (2, 2, 2, 2, 2, 2, 3, 3, 3, 3, 3, 3, 3) sts before last gap, turn; (RS) yo, knit to end.
Rep *short row two* 8 (8, 6, 3, 2, 2, 0, 10, 9, 10, 8, 5, 4, 1) more time(s).
Next row *short row 3:* (WS) Knit to 3 (3, 3, 3, 3, 3, 3, 4, 4, 4, 4, 4, 4, 4) sts before last gap, turn; (RS) yo, knit to end.
Rep *short row three* 0 (1, 3, 6, 7, 8, 10, 0, 1, 1, 3, 6, 7, 10) more time(s).

Resolve short rows

Next row: (WS) K17 (17, 17, 17, 18, 18, 18, 18, 19, 19, 19, 19, 20, 20), place sts just worked onto waste yarn for collar, then knit to end, working ssk to join each yarnover with the st after gap.
Break yarn.

Back

Return sts held for back to circ.
Next row *pick-up row:* (RS) With RS of back facing and beg at right armhole edge, pick up and knit 5 sts in underarm CO from right front, knit across back sts, then pick up and knit 5 sts in underarm CO from left front—68 (74, 78, 84, 88, 94, 98, 104, 108, 114, 118, 124, 128, 134) sts on needle.
Place a locking st marker into first st of this row for counting.
Cont in garter st until back meas same number of rows as right front to marker for counting, ending after a WS row.

Place a locking st marker for neck on either side of center 20 (20, 20, 20, 22, 22, 22, 22, 24, 24, 24, 24, 26, 26) sts.

Begin shoulder shaping

Next row *short row 1:* (RS) Knit to last 3 (3, 3, 3, 3, 3, 3, 4, 4, 4, 4, 4, 4, 4) sts, turn; (WS) yo, knit to last 3 (3, 3, 3, 3, 3, 3, 4, 4, 4, 4, 4, 4, 4) sts, turn.
Next row *short row 2:* (RS) Yo, knit to 2 (2, 2, 2, 2, 2, 2, 3, 3, 3, 3, 3, 3, 3) sts before last gap, turn; (WS) yo, knit to 2 (2, 2, 2, 2, 2, 2, 3, 3, 3, 3, 3, 3) sts before last gap, turn.
Rep *short row two* 8 (8, 6, 3, 2, 2, 0, 10, 9, 10, 8, 5, 4, 1) more time(s).
Next row *short row 3:* (RS) Yo, knit to 3 (3, 3, 3, 3, 3, 3, 4, 4, 4, 4, 4, 4, 4) sts before last gap, turn; (WS) yo, knit to 3 (3, 3, 3, 3, 3, 3, 4, 4, 4, 4, 4, 4, 4) sts before last gap, turn.
Rep *short row three* 0 (1, 3, 6, 7, 8, 10, 0, 1, 1, 3, 6, 7, 10) more time(s).
Short rows end at neck markers.

Begin neck shaping and resolve short rows

Next row: (RS) BO all sts to neck m, remove m, k2tog yo with the st after gap, then BO rem neck st, knit to end, working k2tog to join each yarnover with the st after gap.
Break yarn leaving a tail roughly five times the width of the shoulder for finishing. Join yarn at neck edge of right shoulder, ready to work a WS row.
Next row: (WS) Knit to end, working ssk to join each yarnover with the st after gap.
Do not break yarn.

Join shoulders

Place sts held for left and right fronts onto spare circ. With WS of pcs held tog and attached yarn, using the three-needle bind off, BO all sts for left shoulder. With long tail at right armhole edge, rep for right shoulder.

Gently steam block piece.

Sleeves

Note: Sleeve is worked with WS facing so that join between body and sleeve will appear on RS of garment.
Turn pc inside out, so that WS is facing. With double-pointed needles (dpns) and beg at underarm, pick up and knit 24 (25, 26, 27, 28, 29, 30, 31, 31, 32, 32, 33, 33, 34) sts to shoulder seam (1 st in each garter ridge), then pick up and knit 24 (25, 26, 27, 28, 29, 30, 31, 31, 32, 32, 33, 33, 34) stitches to underarm—48 (50, 52, 54, 56, 58, 60, 62, 62, 64, 64, 66, 66, 68) sts on needles. Pm for BOR.
First rnd: Knit.
Next rnd: Purl.
Cont in garter st for 10 more rnds, ending after a purl rnd.

Begin sleeve shaping

Next rnd *dec rnd:* K1, k2tog, knit to last 3 sts, ssk, k1 (2 sts dec'd)—46 (48, 50, 52, 54, 56, 58, 60, 60, 62, 62, 64, 64, 66) sts rem.
Rep *dec rnd* every 10 (8, 8, 8, 8, 8, 8, 8, 8, 8, 8, 6, 6, 6) rnds 6 (7, 8, 9, 9, 10, 11, 12, 12, 12, 12, 13, 13, 14) more times—34 (34, 34, 34, 36, 36, 36, 36, 36, 38, 38, 38, 38, 38) sts rem.

Cont in garter st until sleeve meas 18½ (18½, 18½, 18, 18, 18, 17½, 17½, 17½, 17, 17, 16½, 16½, 16)" [47 (47, 47, 45.5, 45.5, 45.5, 44.5, 44.5, 44.5, 43, 43, 42, 42, 40.5) cm] from pick-up, ending after a purl rnd.
Next rnd: Bind off knitwise.

Collar

Place a locking st marker at center of back neck edge so that 10 (10, 10, 10, 11, 11, 11, 11, 12, 12, 12, 12, 13, 13) BO sts are on either side.

Right front collar

Return sts held for right collar to circ. Join yarn ready to work a WS row.
Next row *inc row:* (WS) K1-f/b, knit to end (1 st inc'd)—18 (18, 18, 18, 19, 19, 19, 19, 20, 20, 20, 20, 21, 21) sts.
Next row: (RS) K17 (17, 17, 17, 18, 18, 18, 18, 19, 19, 19, 19, 20, 20), sl 1 knitwise, insert RH needle knitwise into next bound off neck st so that both legs of the bind-off are on RH needle, then knit the bound off legs together with the slipped stitch, turn.
Next row: Knit to end.
Rep the last two rows until collar reaches center back neck m, ending after a WS row.

Begin short row shaping

Note: There is no need to work wraps or yarnovers for these short rows.
Next row *short row 1:* (RS) Knit to last 6 (6, 6, 6, 7, 7, 7, 7, 7, 7, 7, 7, 7, 7) sts, turn; (WS) knit to end.
Next row *short row 2:* (RS) Knit to 6 (6, 6, 6, 6, 6, 6, 7, 7, 7, 7, 7, 7) sts before last gap, turn; (WS) knit to end.
Break yarn. Place sts onto waste yarn.

Left front collar
Return sts held for left collar to circ. Join yarn, ready to work a RS row.
Next row *inc row:* (RS) K1-f/b, knit to end (1 st inc'd)—18 (18, 18, 18, 19, 19, 19, 19, 20, 20, 20, 20, 21, 21) sts.
Next row: (WS) K17 (17, 17, 17, 18, 18, 18, 18, 19, 19, 19, 19, 20, 20), sl 1 purlwise, insert RH needle knitwise into next bound off neck st so that both legs of the bind-off are on RH needle, then knit the bound off legs together with the slipped stitch, turn.
Next row: Knit to end.
Rep the last two rows until collar reaches center back neck m, ending after a RS row. Remove m.

Begin short row shaping
Next row *short row 1:* (WS) Knit to last 6 (6, 6, 6, 7, 7, 7, 7, 7, 7, 7, 7, 7, 7) sts, turn; (RS) knit to end.
Next row *short row 2:* (WS) Knit to 6 (6, 6, 6, 6, 6, 6, 7, 7, 7, 7, 7, 7) sts before last gap, turn; (RS) knit to end.
Do not break yarn.

Join collar
Place sts held for right collar onto a dpn. With RS of pcs held tog and attached yarn, using the three-needle bind off, BO all sts.

Right gusset
With WS facing, and beg at bottom increase edge of right front, pick up and knit 1 st in front CO edge, then pick up and knit 1 st in each garter ridge to end of increase edge on back, then pick up and knit 1 st in back CO edge—38 (42, 42, 46, 46, 50, 50, 54, 54, 58, 58, 62, 62, 66) sts.
First row: (RS) Knit.
Cont in garter st until gusset meas 3 (3, 3, 4, 4, 4, 5, 5, 5, 6, 6, 6, 7, 7)" [7.5 (7.5, 7.5, 10, 10, 10, 12.5, 12.5, 12.5, 15, 15, 15, 18, 18) cm] (or desired length) from pick-up, ending after a RS row.
Next row: Bind off knitwise.

Left gusset
With WS facing and beg at bottom increase edge of back, pick up and knit 1 st in back CO edge, then pick up and knit 1 st in each garter ridge to end of increase edge on left front, then pick up and knit 1 st in front CO edge—38 (42, 42, 46, 46, 50, 50, 54, 54, 58, 58, 62, 62, 66) sts.
Work left gusset same as for right gusset.

Finishing
Weave in ends. Gently steam block. Sew buttons opposite buttonholes.

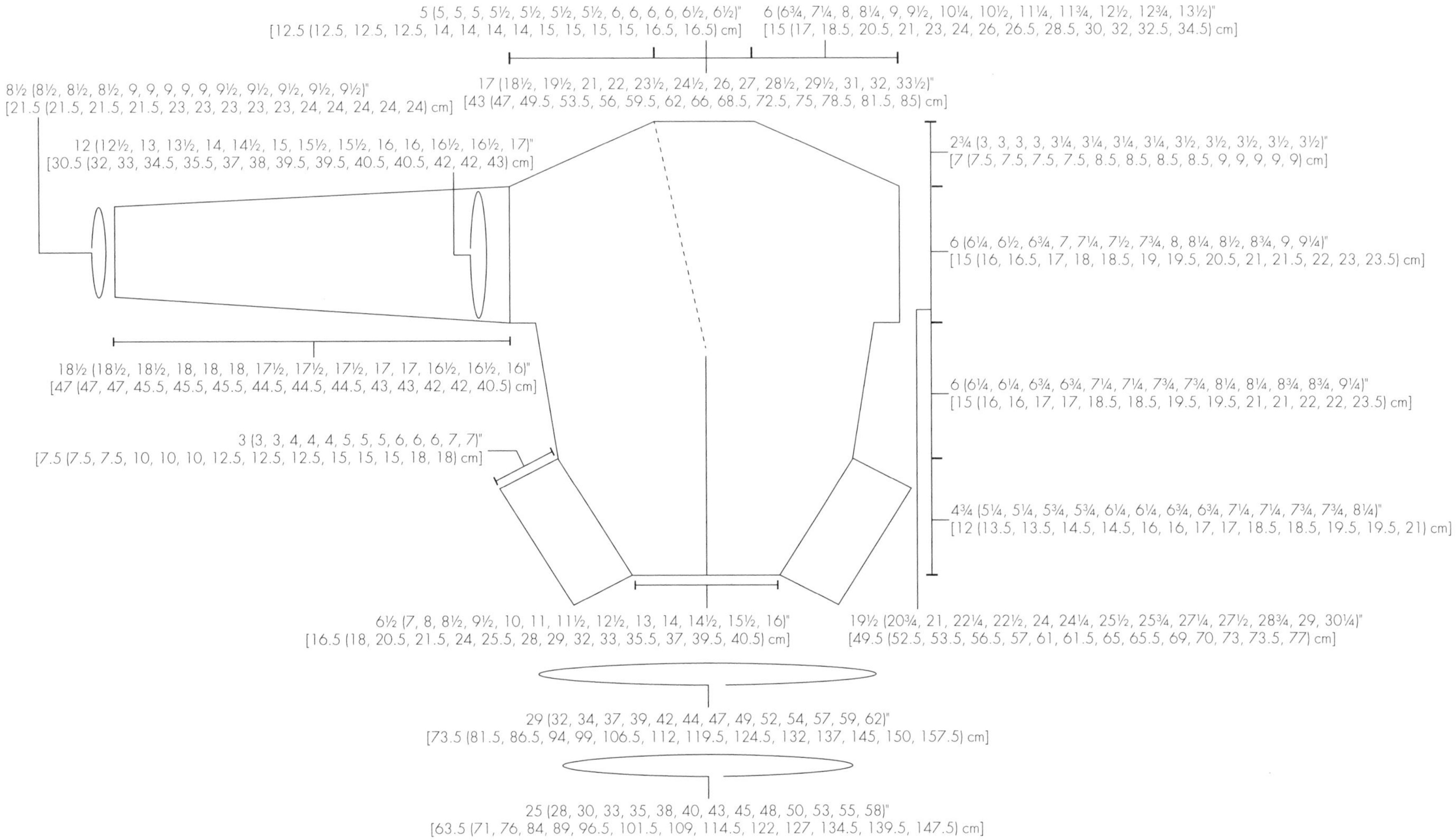
5 (5, 5, 5, 5½, 5½, 5½, 5½, 6, 6, 6, 6, 6½, 6½)"
[12.5 (12.5, 12.5, 12.5, 14, 14, 14, 14, 15, 15, 15, 15, 16.5, 16.5) cm]
6 (6¾, 7¼, 8, 8¼, 9, 9½, 10¼, 10½, 11¼, 11¾, 12½, 12¾, 13½)"
[15 (17, 18.5, 20.5, 21, 23, 24, 26, 26.5, 28.5, 30, 32, 32.5, 34.5) cm]
17 (18½, 19½, 21, 22, 23½, 24½, 26, 27, 28½, 29½, 31, 32, 33½)"
[43 (47, 49.5, 53.5, 56, 59.5, 62, 66, 68.5, 72.5, 75, 78.5, 81.5, 85) cm]
8½ (8½, 8½, 8½, 9, 9, 9, 9, 9, 9½, 9½, 9½, 9½, 9½)"
[21.5 (21.5, 21.5, 21.5, 23, 23, 23, 23, 23, 24, 24, 24, 24, 24) cm]
12 (12½, 13, 13½, 14, 14½, 15, 15½, 15½, 16, 16, 16½, 16½, 17)"
[30.5 (32, 33, 34.5, 35.5, 37, 38, 39.5, 39.5, 40.5, 40.5, 42, 42, 43) cm]
2¾ (3, 3, 3, 3, 3¼, 3¼, 3¼, 3¼, 3½, 3½, 3½, 3½, 3½)"
[7 (7.5, 7.5, 7.5, 7.5, 8.5, 8.5, 8.5, 8.5, 9, 9, 9, 9, 9) cm]
6 (6¼, 6½, 6¾, 7, 7¼, 7½, 7¾, 8, 8¼, 8½, 8¾, 9, 9¼)"
[15 (16, 16.5, 17, 18, 18.5, 19, 19.5, 20.5, 21, 21.5, 22, 23, 23.5) cm]
18½ (18½, 18½, 18, 18, 18, 17½, 17½, 17½, 17, 17, 16½, 16½, 16)"
[47 (47, 47, 45.5, 45.5, 45.5, 44.5, 44.5, 44.5, 43, 43, 42, 42, 40.5) cm]
6 (6¼, 6¼, 6¾, 6¾, 7¼, 7¼, 7¾, 7¾, 8¼, 8¼, 8¾, 8¾, 9¼)"
[15 (16, 16, 17, 17, 18.5, 18.5, 19.5, 19.5, 21, 21, 22, 22, 23.5) cm]
3 (3, 3, 4, 4, 4, 5, 5, 5, 6, 6, 6, 7, 7)"
[7.5 (7.5, 7.5, 10, 10, 10, 12.5, 12.5, 12.5, 15, 15, 15, 18, 18) cm]
4¾ (5¼, 5¼, 5¾, 5¾, 6¼, 6¼, 6¾, 6¾, 7¼, 7¼, 7¾, 7¾, 8¼)"
[12 (13.5, 13.5, 14.5, 14.5, 16, 16, 17, 17, 18.5, 18.5, 19.5, 19.5, 21) cm]
6½ (7, 8, 8½, 9½, 10, 11, 11½, 12½, 13, 14, 14½, 15½, 16)"
[16.5 (18, 20.5, 21.5, 24, 25.5, 28, 29, 32, 33, 35.5, 37, 39.5, 40.5) cm]
19½ (20¾, 21, 22¼, 22½, 24, 24¼, 25½, 25¾, 27¼, 27½, 28¾, 29, 30¼)"
[49.5 (52.5, 53.5, 56.5, 57, 61, 61.5, 65, 65.5, 69, 70, 73, 73.5, 77) cm]
29 (32, 34, 37, 39, 42, 44, 47, 49, 52, 54, 57, 59, 62)"
[73.5 (81.5, 86.5, 94, 99, 106.5, 112, 119.5, 124.5, 132, 137, 145, 150, 157.5) cm]
25 (28, 30, 33, 35, 38, 40, 43, 45, 48, 50, 53, 55, 58)"
[63.5 (71, 76, 84, 89, 96.5, 101.5, 109, 114.5, 122, 127, 134.5, 139.5, 147.5) cm]

snowberry

A jaunty cap, deliberately short, in colors and a kind of colorwork pattern I simply can't get enough of. It would be lovely, too, worked in the gentle palette used in Bayberry.

Finished measurements
17¾ (20)" [45 (51) cm] circumference and 9½ (9¾)" [24 (25) cm] tall, unfolded

Yarn
Owl by Quince & Co
(50% American wool, 50% alpaca; 120yd [110m]/50g)
- 1 (2) skeins Albertine 306 (A)
- 1 skein Allagash 371 (B)
- 1 skein Steppe 327 (C)
- 1 skein Snowy 300 (D)
- 1 skein Barred 307 (E)

Note: Only approx 10-12 yd of B, C, D, and E are used. If you have Owl leftovers, use them!

Needles
- One 16" circular needle (circ) in size US 7 [4.5 mm]
- One 16" circ in size US 9 [5.5 mm]
- One set double-pointed needles (dpns) in size US 7 [4.5 mm]
- One set dpns in size US 9 [5.5 mm]

Or size to obtain gauge

Notions
- Stitch marker
- Tapestry needle

Gauge
17 sts and 23 rnds = 4" [10 cm] in colorwork pattern for swatching with larger needle, after blocking.

Colorwork pattern for swatching (multiple of 20 stitches)
Note: Each smaller motif is a repeat of 4 or 5 stitches, but to get all motifs to end at the same place, we recommend a 20-stitch multiple for swatching.
See also chart, page 110.
Rnd 1: With A, knit.
Rnds 2 and 3: Rep Rnd 1.
Rnd 4: *With B, k2, with A, k3; rep from * to end.
Rnd 5: *With B, k2, with C, p3; rep from * to end.
Rnd 6: *With B, k2, with C, k3; rep from * to end.
Rnd 7: *With D, p2, with C, k3; rep from * to end.
Rnd 8: *With A, k2, with D, p3; rep from * to end.
Rnds 9 and 10: *With A, k2, with D, k3; rep from * to end.
Rnd 11: With A, *k2, p3; rep from * to end.
Rnds 12 and 13: With A, knit.
Rnd 14: *With A, k1, with E, k2, with A, k1; rep from * to end.
Rnd 15: *With A, k1, p2, k1; rep from * to end.
Rnds 16 and 17: With A, knit.
Rnds 18 and 19: *With A, k2, with B, k2; rep from * to end.
Rnd 20: With D, *k2, p2; rep from * to end.
Rnd 21: *With D, k2, with A, k2; rep from * to end.
Rnd 22: *With C, p2, with A, k2; rep from * to end.
Rnds 23 and 24: With A, knit.

hat

With A, smaller circular needle (circ) and using the long-tail cast on, CO 94 (108) sts. Place marker for beg of rnd and join to work in the rnd, careful not to twist sts.

Begin rib

First rnd: *K1, p1; rep from * to end of rnd.
Cont in est rib for 3¾ (4)" [9.5 (10) cm].
Change to larger circ.

Begin stockinette stitch

Next rnd *dec rnd:* *K3, k2tog, k2, k2tog, k3, ssk, k4 (2), ssk; rep from * to last 14 (18) sts, k3 (4), k2tog, k2 (4), k2tog, k3 (4), ssk; 19 (23) sts dec'd)—75 (85) sts rem.
Next 3 rnds: Knit.

Begin colorwork

See also Chart 1, page 110.
Rnd 1: *With B, k2, with A, k3; rep from * to end.
Rnd 2: *With B, k2, with C, p3; rep from * to end.
Rnd 3: *With B, k2, with C, k3; rep from * to end.
Rnd 4: *With D, p2, with C, k3; rep from * to end.
Rnd 5: *With A, k2, with D, p3; rep from * to end.
Rnds 6 and 7: *With A, k2, with D, k3; rep from * to end.
Rnd 8: With A, *k2, p3; rep from * to end.
Rnd 9: With A, knit.

Size 17¾ (-)" [45 (-) cm] only:
Next rnd *dec rnd:* With A, *k23, k2tog; rep from * two more times to end (3 sts dec'd)—72 sts rem.
Proceed to All sizes.

Size - (20)" [- (51) cm] only:
Next rnd *dec rnd:* With A, k42, k2tog, knit to end (1 st dec'd)—84 sts rem.

All sizes

Break B, C, and D.

Continue colorwork

See also Chart 2, page 110.
Rnd 1: *With A, k1, with E, k2, with A, k1; rep from * to end.
Rnd 2: *With A, k1, p2, k1; rep from * to end.
Rnd 3: With A, knit.
Break E.

Begin crown shaping

Note: Change to larger double-pointed needles (dpns) when necessary.
Next rnd *dec rnd:* With A, *k4 (5), k2tog; rep from * to end (12 sts dec'd)—60 (72) sts rem.

End colorwork

See also Chart 3, page 110.
Rnds 1 and 2: *With A, k2, with B, k2; rep from * to end.
Rnd 3: With D, *k2, p2; rep from * to end.
Rnd 4: *With D, k2, with A, k2; rep from * to end.
Rnd 5: *With C, p2, with A, k2; rep from * to end.
Rnd 6: With A, knit.
Next rnd *dec rnd:* With A, *k1, k2tog; rep from * to end; 20 (24) sts dec'd—40 (48) sts rem.
Change to smaller dpns. Break B, C, and D. Continue with A only.

Begin ribbed crown

Next rnd: With A, *k1, p1; rep from * to end.
Cont in rib for 5 more rnds.
Next rnd *dec rnd:* *K3tog, p1; rep from * to end; 20 (24) sts dec'd—20 (24) sts rem.
Cont in rib for 4 more rnds.

Size 17¾ (-)" [45 (-) cm] only:
Next rnd: *K2tog; rep from * to end (10 sts dec'd)—10 sts rem.
Proceed to All sizes.

Size - (20)" [- (51) cm] only:
Next rnd: *K3tog; rep from * to end (16 sts dec'd)—8 sts rem.

All sizes

Break yarn leaving approx 12" [30.5 cm] tail. With tapestry needle, draw tail through rem sts. Cinch closed.

Finishing

Weave in ends. Gently steam block, if desired.

Key

- knit with specified color
- • purl with specified color
- with A, work as specified
- with B, work as specified
- with C, work as specified
- with D, work as specified
- + with E, work as specified

Chart 1

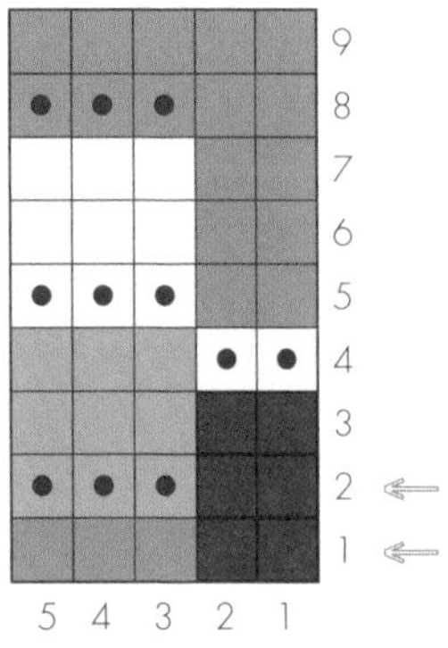

Chart 2

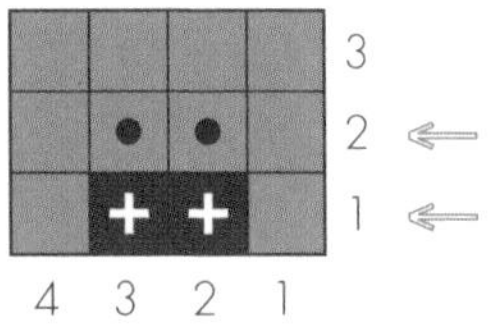

Chart 3

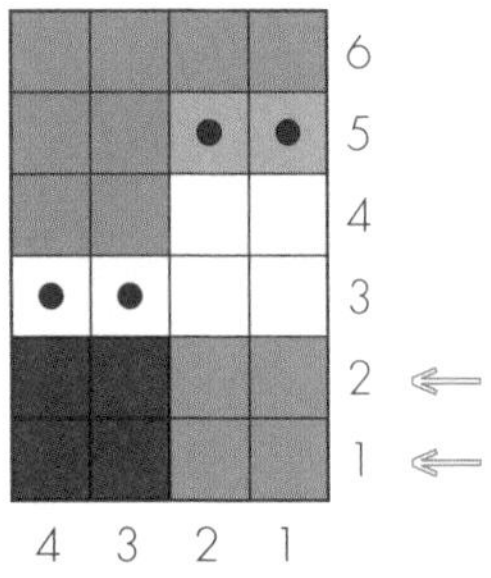

Chart for gauge swatch

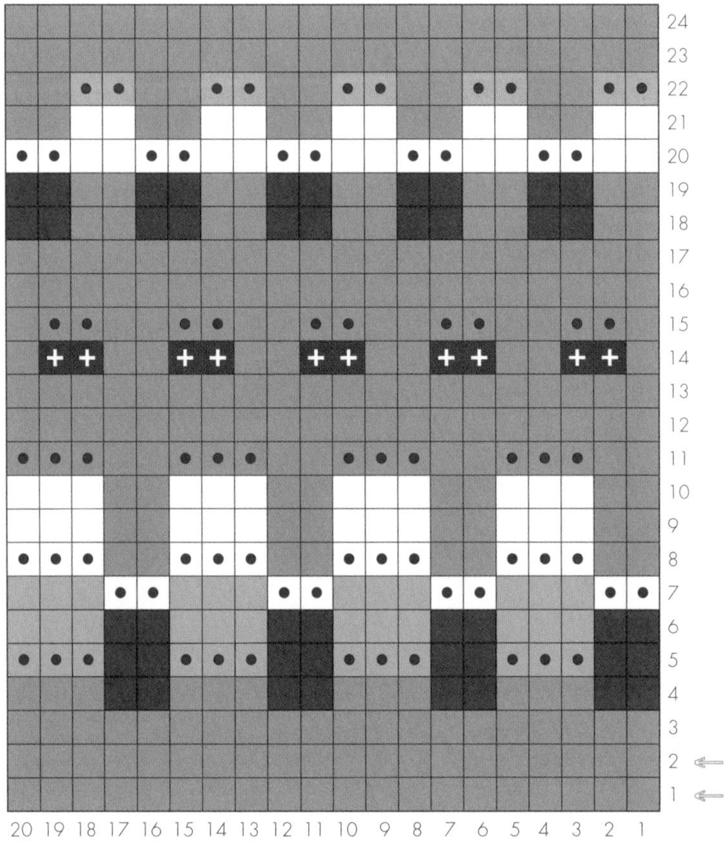

stitches & techniques

stockinette stitch (St st)

Flat
Knit on the RS, purl on the WS.
In the round
Knit every round.

reverse stockinette stitch (rev St st)

Flat
Purl on the RS, knit on the WS.
In the round
Purl every round.

garter stitch

Flat
Knit every row.
In the round
Rnd 1: Knit.
Rnd 2: Purl.
Repeat Rnds 1 and 2 for garter stitch.

making a slipknot

If beginning a long-tail cast on, from the tail end of your yarn ball, measure out about an inch for every stitch you'll cast on, and a few extra inches for good measure. If working another type of cast on, a 6-8" [15-20 cm] tail will suffice.
At this point on your strand, make your first stitch, a slipknot, to secure the yarn to the needle.

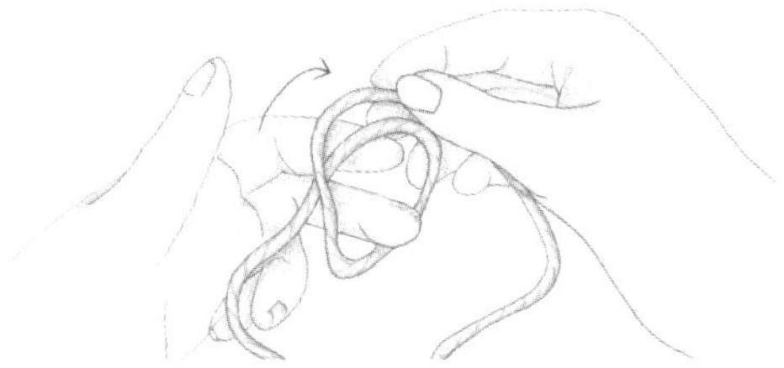

Make a smallish loop, about the size of a silver dollar, overlapping the tail end on the working yarn.

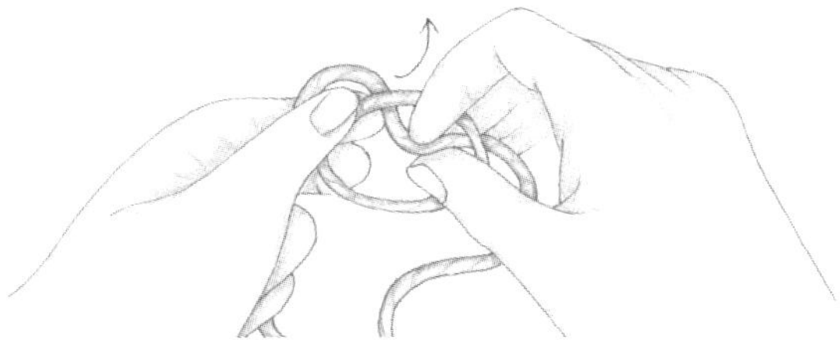

Reach through the loop and grab the tail.

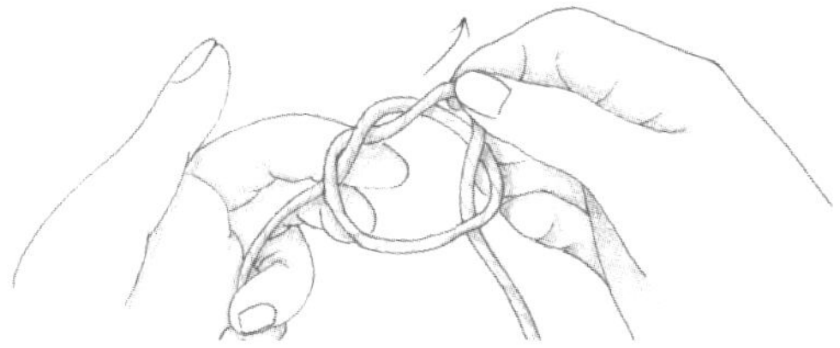

Pull it through the loop.

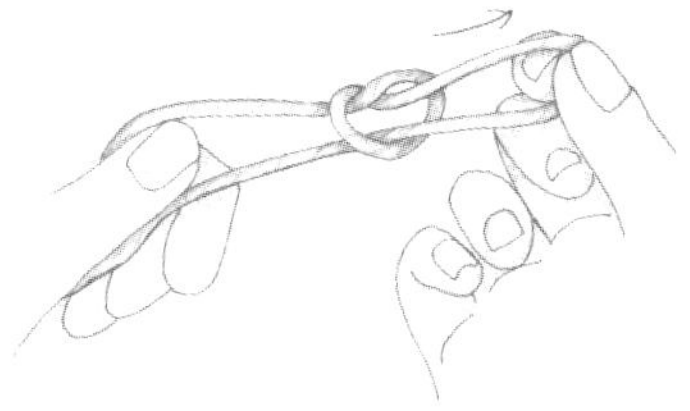

Holding the loop just pulled through, pull gently on the yarn ends until the pulled-loop shrinks a little. This is your slipknot.

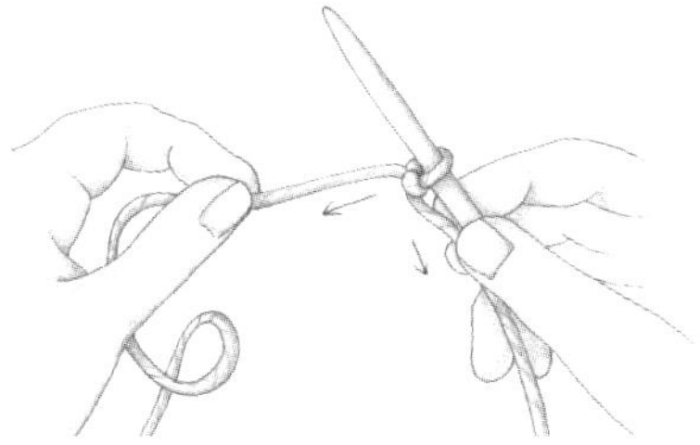

Put the slipknot on your needle. Snug the knot by gently pulling on both ends.

long-tail cast on

Begin the long-tail cast on by making a slipknot.

Take a look at the strands hanging from the slipknot snugged on your needle. The working yarn is the end that comes from your ball.

Position the strands so the working yarn is on the right and the tail is on the left.

Hold the needle and the working yarn in your right hand, the tail in your left, a few inches away from the needle, with a little tension on it and thumb on top of yarn.

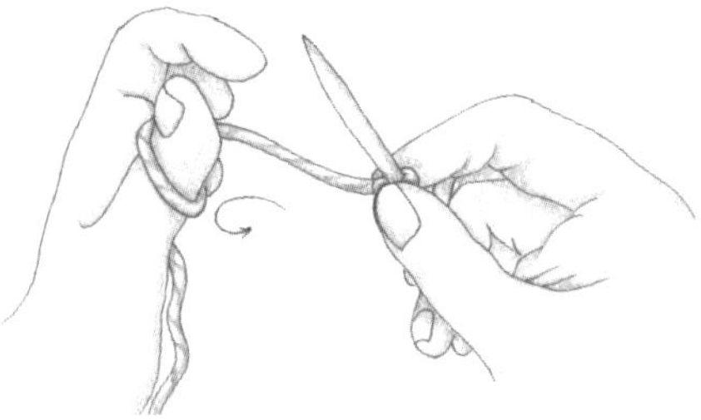

Create a loop by rotating your thumb under the tail end from behind, then up so your thumb is parallel with the needle and the yarn is looped around it.

Insert the tip of the needle upward into the loop formed around your thumb.

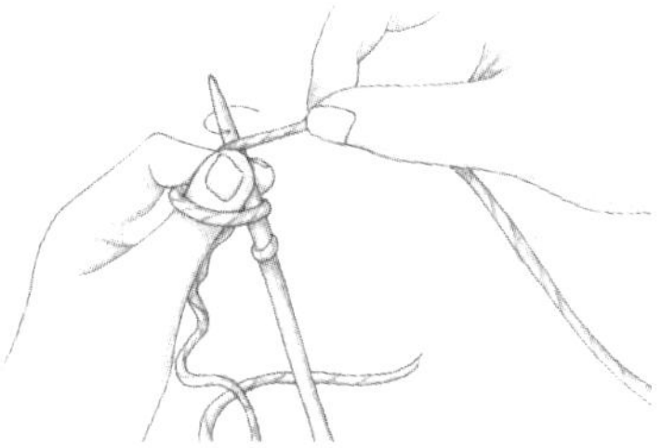

Secure this position by switching the needle to your left hand while it's still in the loop on your thumb and, with your right hand, wrap the working yarn counter-clockwise around the needle and sandwich it between the thumb and the needle in your left hand.

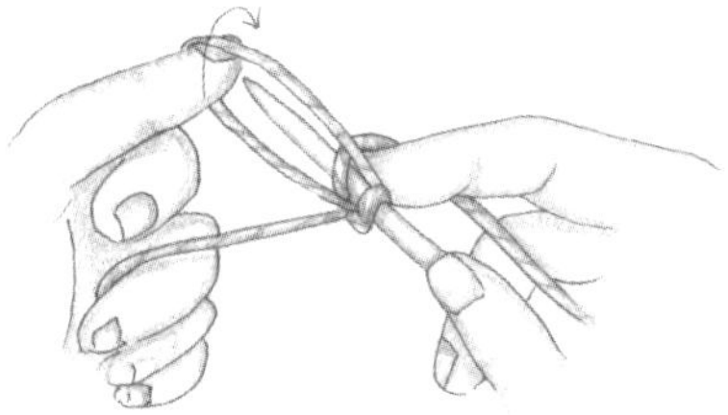

Now, grasp the needle again with your right hand and with your thumb lift the loop of yarn that's been sitting on it, bring it up and back and over the tip of the needle.

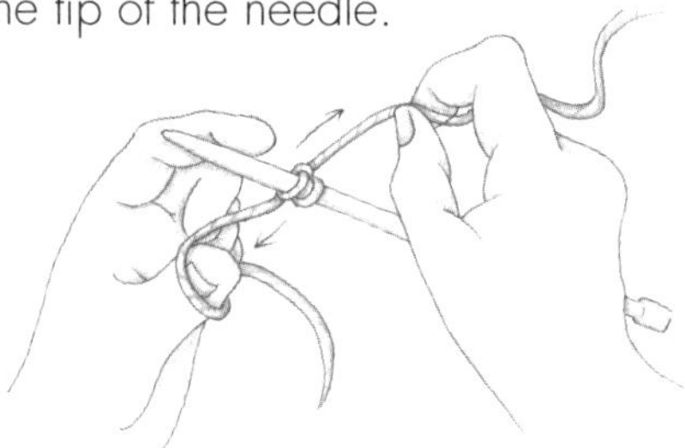

Repeat until you have cast on the number of stitches you need (remember: the slipknot counts as your first stitch).

yarnover short rows

In stockinette or reverse stockinette stitch with knit side facing

Knit to the point where the short row begins. Turn work.

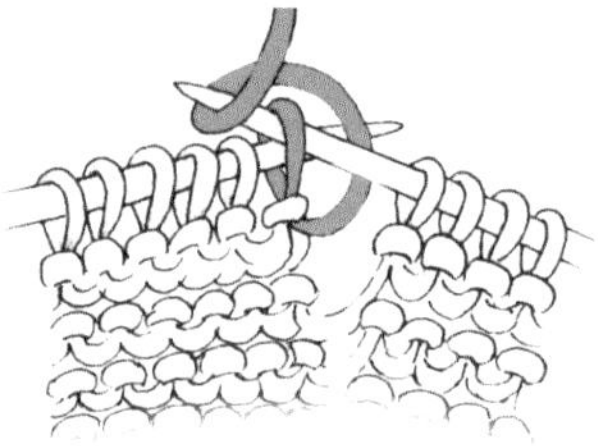

fig 1

With purl side now facing, bring yarn between needles to the back and behind the RH needle, purl the first stitch on the LH needle so that yarn travels up and over the RH needle, creating a yarnover beside the stitch just worked (fig 1). You are now ready to purl back along your short row.

In stockinette or reverse stockinette stitch with purl side facing

Purl to the point where the short row begins. Turn work.

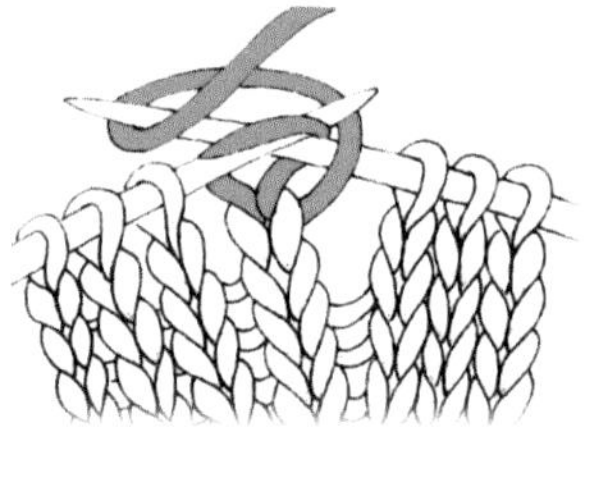

fig 2

With the knit side now facing, bring yarn to the front between needles and in front of RH needle, knit the first stitch on the LH needle so that the yarn travels up and over the RH needle, creating a yarnover beside the stitch just worked (fig 2). You are now ready to knit back along your short row.

In garter stitch, RS or WS facing
Knit to the point where the short row begins. Turn work.
With the opposite side now facing, leave yarn in front of work and RH needle, then knit the first stitch on the LH needle creating a yarnover next to the stitch just worked. You are now ready to knit back along your short row.

Working in a stitch pattern
For both right side and wrong side rows, continuing in stitch pattern when possible, work to the point where the short row begins. Turn work.

If the first stitch is a knit stitch, a brk, or a sl 1 or sl1yo that resembles the V of a knit stitch, bring yarn to the front between needles, then work the stitch, forming the yarnover beside it.

If the first stitch is a purl stitch, a brp, or a sl 1 or sl1yo that resembles the ridge of a purl stitch, bring yarn to the back between needles, then work the stitch, forming the yarnover beside it.

resolving short rows

After completing your short rows, each yarnover is decreased with the stitch that follows the gap created by the turn. The decrease used to close the gaps will make these short rows invisible on the right side, regardless of whether they are knit stitches or purls.

If resolving with knit st on RS
On the knit side (RS), knit to the yarnover (at right edge of gap) (fig 3), then k2tog the yarnover with the stitch after gap (fig 4). Repeat for each yarnover as you work to the end of the row.

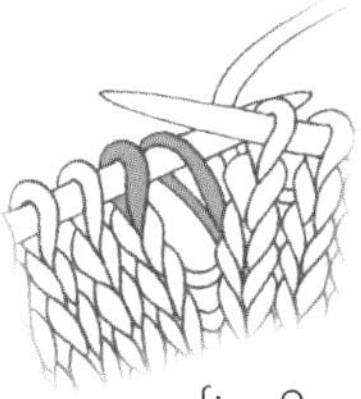
fig 3

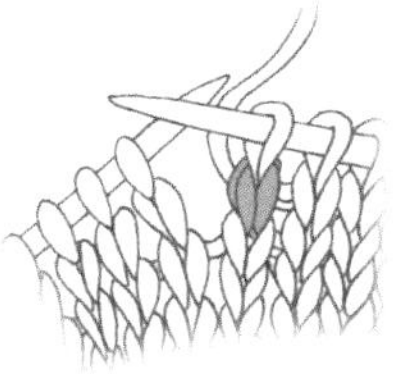
fig 4

If resolving with purl st on WS
On the purl side (WS), purl to the yarnover (at right edge of gap) (fig 5), then ssp the yarnover with the stitch after gap (fig 6). Repeat for each yarnover as you work to the end of the row.

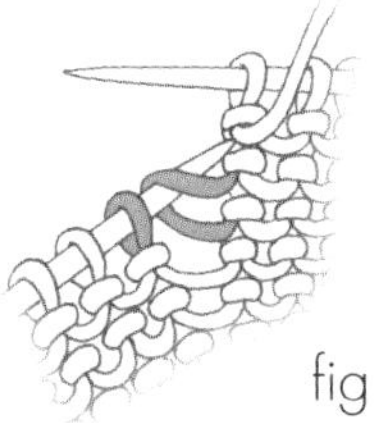
fig 5

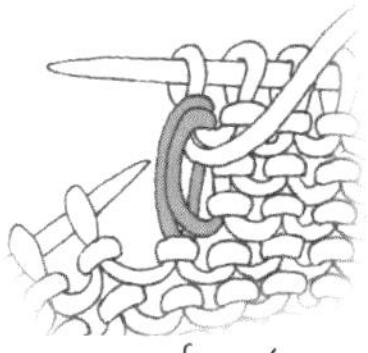
fig 6

If resolving with purl st on RS
On the purl side (RS), purl to the yarnover (at right edge of gap), then p2tog the yarnover with the stitch after gap (fig 7). Repeat for each yarnover as you work to the end of the row.

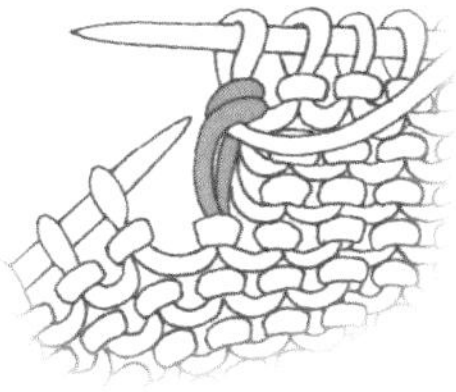
fig 7

If resolving with knit st on WS
On the knit side (WS), knit to the yarnover (at right edge of gap), then ssk the yarnover with the stitch after gap (fig 8). Repeat for each yarnover as you work to the end of the row.

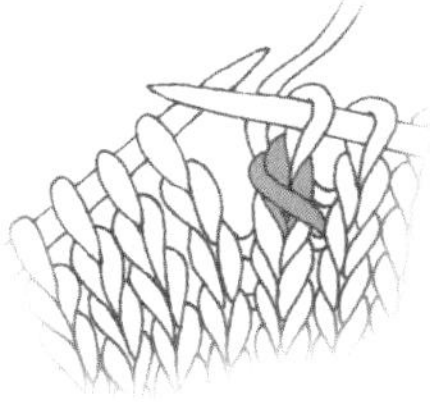
fig 8

In garter stitch
On the RS, knit to the yarnover (at right edge of gap), then k2tog the yarnover with the stitch after gap. Repeat for each yarnover as you work to the end of the row.

On the WS, knit to the yarnover, then ssk the yarnover with the stitch after gap. Repeat for each yarnover as you work to the end of the row.

beginning a sleeve from a waste yarn cast on

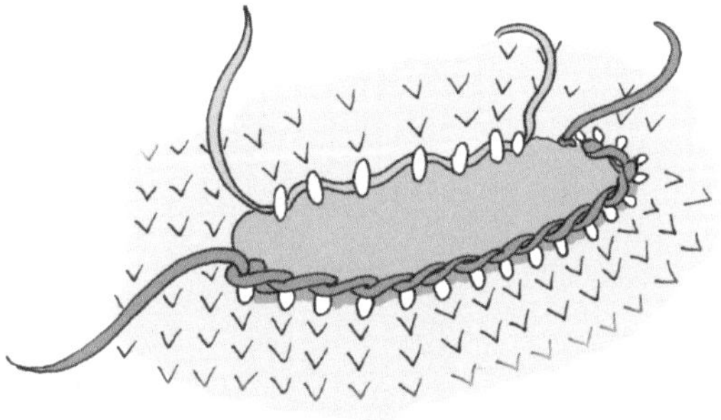

Place your sweater with the sleeve opening laid out flat before you, so that the waste yarn cast on is facing up.

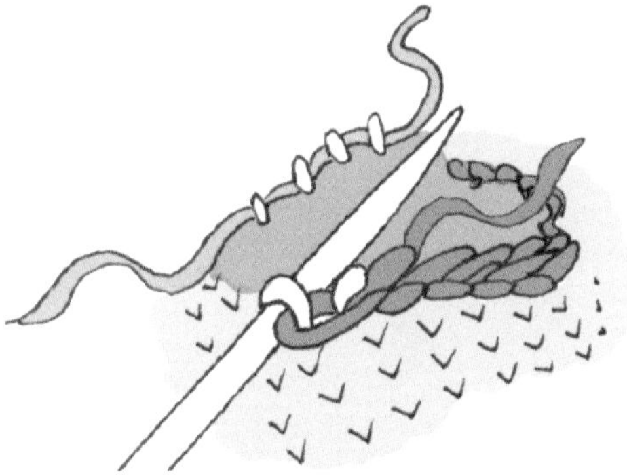

Insert needle tip from front to back into the first stitch (waste yarn is coming from the center of the stitch).

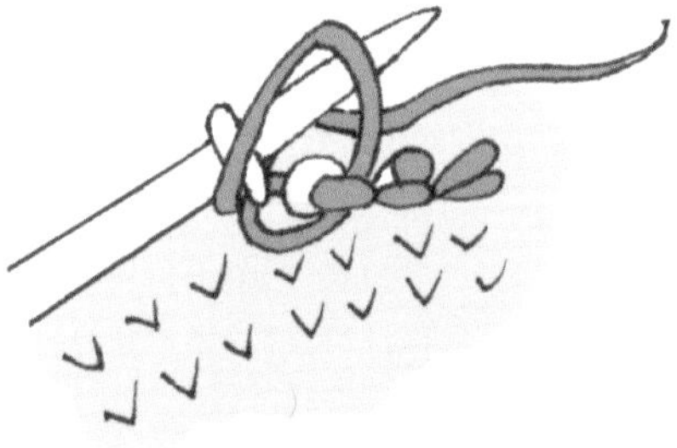

Carefully pick the waste yarn out of the stitch just placed on needle, drawing the tail first back through the stitch to the right,

then down from the center of the next cast on stitch,

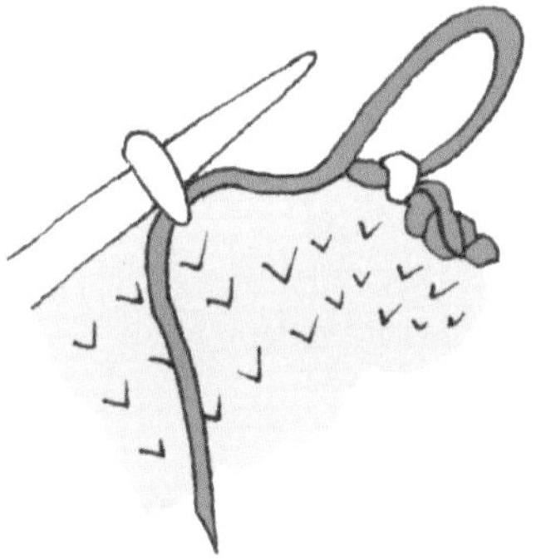

and finally through the stitch again, this time to the left, until it is completely removed from the stitch.

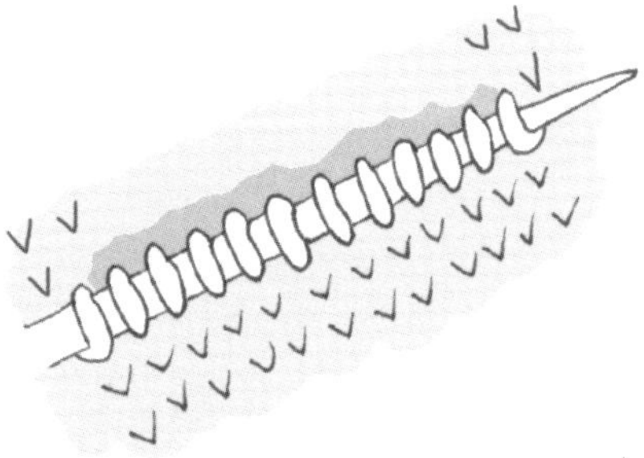

Continue in this manner, one stitch at a time, until all stitches have been placed on needle and waste yarn is removed completely.

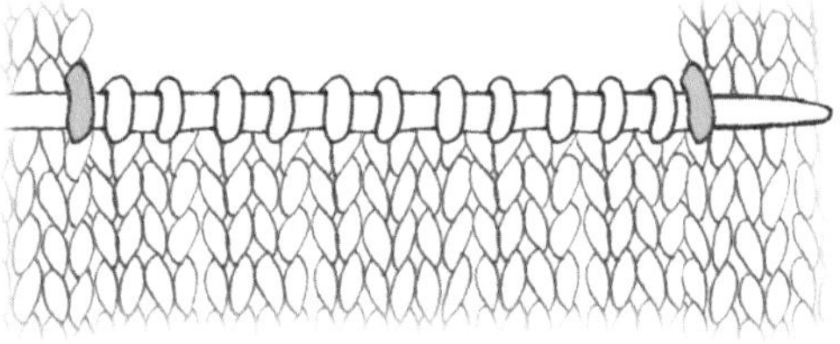

There will be one more stitch on the needle than the number of stitches you cast on. This is because the first and last stitch cast on each "borrow" a leg from a stitch that continued on when working from the body into the yoke on your sweater.

For great illustrated tutorials on the following techniques, visit our blog, quinceandco.com/blogs/news/tagged/techniques

long-tail, backward loop, and cable cast ons

basic and three-needle bind off

picking up stitches

cables with and without a cable needle

speed swatching for colorwork

Visit paper-tiger.net for great tutorials on the following colorwork techniques:

tension

color dominance

standard abbreviations

approx	approximately
beg	begin(ning); begin(s)
BO	bind off
BOR	beginning of round
CO	cast on
circ	circular needle
cm	centimeter(s)
cn	cable needle
cont	continue(s); continuing
dec('d)	decrease(d)
dpn(s)	double-pointed needle(s)
est	establish(ed)
g	gram(s)
inc('d)	increase(d)
k	knit
LH	left hand
meas	measures
mm	millimeter(s)
m	marker(s)
p	purl
patt(s)	pattern(s)
pc(s)	piece(s)
pm	place marker
psso	pass slipped stitch(es) over
rem	remain(ing); remain(s)
rep	repeat(ing); repeat(s)
RH	right hand
rib	ribbing
rnd(s)	round(s)
RS	right side
sl	slip
sl m	slip marker
st(s)	stitch(es)
St st	stockinette stitch
tog	together
WS	wrong side
yd	yard(s)

special abbreviations

brk (brioche knit): Knit the next stitch together with its yo.

C4B (cable 4 back, leans to the right): Slip 2 stitches onto cable needle (cn) and hold in back, k2, then k2 from cn.

C4F (cable 4 front, leans to the left): Slip 2 stitches onto cn and hold in front, k2, then k2 from cn.

C6B (cable 6 back, leans to the right): Slip 3 stitches onto cn and hold in back, k3, then k3 from cn.

C6F (cable 6 front, leans to the left): Slip 3 stitches onto cn and hold in front, k3, then k3 from cn.

k1-f/b (knit 1, front and back): Knit into the front loop, then the back loop, of next stitch (1 stitch increased).

k2tog: Knit 2 stitches together (1 stitch decreased, leans to the right).

k3tog: Knit 3 stitches together (2 stitches decreased, leans to the right).

LT (left twist): Skip 1 stitch and knit the next stitch through the back loop (tbl) keeping both stitches on needle, knit the skipped stitch, then slip both stitches from needle together.

M1R (make 1 right slanting): Insert LH needle from back to front under horizontal strand between stitch just worked and next stitch, knit lifted strand through the front loop (1 stitch increased).

M1L (make 1 left slanting): Insert LH needle from front to back under horizontal strand between stitch just worked and next stitch, knit lifted strand through the back loop (1 stitch increased).

m1-L/loop: Wrap yarn around your left thumb from back to front—tail will be at front of your thumb, closest to you. Secure tail in palm with other fingers. Insert RH needle tip upward from below the yarn tail, through loop wrapped around thumb. Remove your thumb and pull yarn to tighten (1 stitch increased).

m1-p/R (make 1 purlwise right slanting): Insert LH needle from back to front under horizontal strand between stitch just worked and next stitch, purl lifted strand through the front loop (1 stitch increased).

m1-p/L (make 1 purlwise left slanting): Insert LH needle from front to back under horizontal strand between stitch just worked and next stitch, purl lifted strand through the back loop (1 stitch increased).

p2tog: Purl 2 stitches together (1 stitch decreased).

p3tog: Purl 3 stitches together (2 stitches decreased).

p3tog-tbl: Purl 3 stitches together through the back loops (2 stitches decreased).

RT (right twist): Skip 1 stitch and knit the next stitch, knit the skipped stitch, then slip both stitches from needle.

sk2p: Slip 1 stitch knitwise to RH needle, k2tog, pass slipped stitch over stitch created by k2tog (2 stitches decreased, leans to the left).

sl1yo (slip 1 yarn over): Bring the yarn to the front, between the needles, then slip the next stitch purlwise. Bring the yarn over the needle, to the back, ready to knit the next stitch (creates a yarn over traveling over a slipped stitch).

ssk (slip, slip, knit): Slip 2 stitches one at a time knitwise to the RH needle; return stitches to LH needle in turned position and knit them together through the back loops (1 stitch decreased, leans to the left).

ssp (slip, slip, purl): Slip 2 stitches one at a time knitwise to the RH needle; return stitches to LH needle in turned position and purl them together through the back loops (1 stitch decreased).

yo (yarn over): Bring yarn between needles to the front, then over RH needle ready to knit the next stitch (1 stitch increased).

history & bio

Quince & Co is a handknitting yarn and knitwear design company launched in 2010 by Pam Allen in partnership with a historic spinning mill in Maine. Quince now spins yarn in five different mills in the US and works as much as possible with American fibers. When we can't have a yarn made to our specifications in the US, we look for suppliers overseas who make yarn in as earth- and labor-friendly a way as possible.

Quince began with a core line of five wool yarns—Finch, Chickadee, Lark, Osprey, and Puffin—each with its own personality, each in 37 colors, and all spun in the US from American wool. Today Quince & Co's core line comes in more than 60 colors and we've added Tern, a silk/wool blend, Owl and Owlet, two alpaca/wool blends, Piper and Crane, two super fine mohair/merino blends, Willet and Whimbrel, organic cotton yarns sourced in the US, and Phoebe, an extrafine merino. In addition, Quince works with an Italian mill to make two organic linen yarns, Sparrow and Kestrel. Find out more at www.quinceandco.com.

Pam Allen has worked in the knitting industry for many years as an independent hand-knitwear designer, editor-in-chief of *Interweave Knits* magazine, and as creative director at Quince & Company. She is the author of *Knitting for Dummies* (John Wiley & Sons, 2002), *Home: 18 Knittable Projects to Keep You Comfy* (Quince & Co, 2014), and *Plain & Simple* (Quince & Co, 2017).

acknowledgements

Many thanks to:
Abby Ruskansky-Johnson for photos,
Susan Steller for managing the photo shoot,
Anne Harrison for modeling,
Mark Rockwood for use of Studio 438 as location,
Leila Raven for illustrations,
Bristol Ivy for proofreading,
Dawn Catanzaro, Jerusha Neely, Minh Nguyen, and Marie Horner for general production of the book,
Dawn Catanzaro and Hallie Ojala-Barrett for sample kntting,
Ali R, Annette M, Betsy I, Christine P, Elisabeth B, Glenna C, Jody F, Marie H, Michael S, Rachael R, Renee O, Sandi P, Thomas F, TingTing L, Tracey C, Yvonne M for pattern testing,
Ryan FitzGerald for encouraging the book,
and to all the smart, talented, dedicated, and hardworking people at Quince & Company for making it the company it is.

Notes

Notes

Notes